MEDELLÍN TRAVEL GUIDE 2024

Unveiling Hidden Gems, Insider Tips, and Cultural Treasures in Colombia's Vibrant City

By

Nola M. Garcia

Table of Contents

INTRODUCTION

Medellin: My enchanting journey

Setting off on a trip to Medellin was an adventure of deep experiences, self-discovery, and cultural absorption rather than merely seeing a new place. The trip started months in advance of actually setting foot in Colombia, including months of careful preparation, reading up, and waiting.

It seemed like entering into a colorful tapestry of colors, noises, and smells when I arrived in Medellin. The vibrant streets were alive with activity, throbbing to the beat of salsa music and the voices of neighborhood residents. Every encounter was surrounded by the warmth of Colombian hospitality, which overcame communication gaps and created bonds that cut across cultural divides.

We spent days seeing everything that the city has to offer, from the breathtaking views of Parque Arví to the architectural wonders of Plaza Botero. From its turbulent past to its robust present, Medellin's rich history and culture were unveiled in every corner.

Exploring the outskirts of the city revealed the astounding natural splendor of Colombia. It was like walking into a storybook as we made our way into the foggy mountains of Cocora Valley, which is home to enormous wax palms. Climbing the recognizable El Peñol Rock provided expansive vistas of Guatapé's winding lakes and lush hillsides, illustrating the nation's variety of topography.

However, seeing everyday living and not simply tourism was what made the trip really meaningful. It became a gastronomic expedition in and of itself to sample typical Colombian treats like the savory arepas and the hearty bandeja paisa. Speaking with people, whether in limited Spanish or via gestures, provided insights into their aspirations, challenges, and daily lives.

Days became weeks, and then months, and Medellin started to feel like home. Giving back to the community that had welcomed you so warmly may take the form of helping out at local organizations, teaching English to enthusiastic students, or just being there to offer a helping hand when required.

About Medellin

The dynamic city of Medellin, which is tucked away in Colombia's Aburrá Valley, has become a top choice for tourists looking for a unique fusion of local culture, historical sites, and scenic views. Many factors combine to make Medellin a popular travel destination worldwide, including its good environment, hospitable residents, and vibrant atmosphere.

1. Resilience and Transformation: Previously known as the "most dangerous city in the world," Medellin has seen a notable metamorphosis in the last few years. The city has reborn itself as a lighthouse of ingenuity, inventiveness, and tenacity, emerging from the ashes of its stormy history like a phoenix. Visitors are attracted to Comuna 13, which was once known for violence but has now evolved into a thriving center of art and community, to see this amazing development firsthand.

2. Creative Urban Design: Medellin has won praise from all around the world for its dedication to inclusive urban development. In addition to providing effective transportation, the city's well-known Metrocable system—a network of cable cars that connects hillside districts to the city center—also promotes social integration and economic opportunity for underprivileged groups. Visitors swarm to see this avant-garde method of urban design and take in the stunning aerial vistas of the metropolis.

3. Cultural Riches: From its well-known festivals honoring music, dance, and folklore to its top-notch museums and galleries, Medellin pulsates with a rich tapestry of cultural traditions. Immerse yourself in the artistic creations of the region's artists at the Museo de Antioquia, which has a sizable collection of the well-known paintings and sculptures of Fernando Botero. The vibrant nightlife of the city provides

many chances for dancing, mingling, and enjoying Colombia's renowned aguardiente. It is concentrated around the pubs and clubs of El Poblado and Laureles.

4. Natural Beauty: Medellin is surrounded by green landscapes and lush mountains, creating a spectacular natural backdrop that appeals to both nature lovers and adventure enthusiasts. Within the city borders, there are many of options to get back in touch with nature, from the serene gardens of Parque Explora to the picturesque trails of Parque Arví. Day visits to neighboring sights like the vibrant town of Guatapé, home to a large reservoir and recognizable rock formation, provide even more chances for exploration and adventure.

5. Gourmet Delights: Medellin has a mouthwatering selection of delectable Colombian dishes to entice the senses. Colombian cuisine is a feast for the senses. Tourists enjoy local favorites like arepas and empanadas, as well as traditional fare like bandeja paisa, a filling buffet of rice, beans, plantains, and meats. Upscale eateries highlight the inventiveness of Medellin's developing culinary scene, while street food sellers cover the city's streets, providing a delectable selection of snacks and delicacies.

In summary, travelers are drawn to Medellin by its alluring fusion of natural beauty, history, and culture. They are encouraged to stroll about the city, interact with locals, and experience the lively energy that sets this place apart from others. Travelers visiting Medellin are certain to have an unforgettable experience, whether they are looking for adventure, leisure, or cultural immersion.

Discover the Unique Culture of Medellin

Medellin is well known for its thriving cultural scene, and the city comes to life every year with a variety of festivals and events that highlight its rich history, music, and food. Here is a thorough rundown of some of the biggest celebrations along with their dates:

1. Festival of Flowers, or Feria de las Flores
- Date: 10 days in early August
One of the most recognizable events in Medellin is Feria de las Flores, which honors the region's rich floral legacy. The Desfile de Silleteros, or Parade of the Silleteros, is the festival's main attraction. Local farmers parade through Medellin's streets with ornately designed flower arrangements slung on their backs. The festival draws visitors from all over the globe with its array of cultural activities, concerts, dance performances, and flower shows.

2. International Tango Festival, or Festival Internacional de Tango
- Date: 10 days in June and July
The International Tango Festival brings together dancers, musicians, and enthusiasts from all over the world to celebrate the passionate dance art of tango. The event includes contests, seminars, milongas (dance parties), and concerts by well-known tango performers. Travelers may take in the sensual beats and complex dance moves of tango while taking in the vibrant energy of Medellin's tango scene.

3. The Festival of Lights, or Festival de la Luz
- Time: The beginning of December
- Description: Medellin's Festival de la Luz ushers in the Christmas season by turning the city into a stunning display of

color and lights. The celebration begins with a large procession that winds through Medellin's downtown streets and includes lit floats, marching bands, dancers, and fireworks. During this enchanting time of year, visitors may marvel at the intricate light displays, street performances, and joyous ambiance that pervades the city.

4. International Jazz Festival, or Festival Internacional de Jazz)
- September
- Held at many locations across Medellin, the International Jazz Festival highlights the varied skills of jazz artists from all over the globe. The festival presents a diverse roster of performances, jam sessions, and seminars that appeal to jazz fans of all ages and preferences, ranging from soothing melodies to improvisational jams. Travelers may take in the dynamic energy of Medellin's music culture while listening to the beautiful sounds of jazz.

5. The Candelaria Virgin's Day Festa de la Virgen de la Candelaria
- Day: Tuesday, February
- Description: Medellin's patron saint is honored on the Feast of the Virgin of Candelaria, a religious occasion. Mass at the Metropolitan Cathedral starts the day, and then processions through the streets with traditional music, dance, and fireworks follow. Traveling great distances to honor the Virgin, pilgrims offer prayers for protection and blessings for themselves and their loved ones.

These are just a few of the many festivals and events that Medellin hosts all year long. Every event provides guests with a singular chance to fully engage with the culture, customs, and joie de vivre of the city, making lifelong memories.

Medellin Time Zone

Colombian Time (COT), observed in Medellin, is in the UTC-5 Time Zone (Coordinated Universal Time minus 5 hours). This is a thorough summary of Medellin's time zone:

1. UTC Offset:
- Coordinated Universal Time (UTC) is five hours behind Medellin's time zone, which is UTC-5. Colombia does not alter its clocks for daylight saving time (DST), hence the offset stays constant all year long.

2. Time Standard:
- Colombian Standard Time (COT), which is equivalent to UTC-5, is observed year-round in Medellin. This implies that in Medellin, it is 7:00 AM while it is 12:00 PM (noon) UTC.

3. Daylight Saving Time
- Colombia does not follow daylight saving time, in contrast to several other nations. As a result, Medellin's time does not change for daylight saving time; it stays the same all year round.

4. Place of Origin:
- Medellin is located in Colombia's Andes Mountains, in the Aburrá Valley, at an altitude of around 1,500 meters (4,900 feet) above sea level. Due to its physical position inside the UTC-5 time zone, it shares the same time zone as other major Colombian cities like Cali and Bogotá.

5. Time Zone Delimitations:
- The UTC-5 time zone, also referred to as Colombia Time (COT), encompasses a large portion of South America, including Ecuador, Peru, and Colombia. Because all of Colombia is in the same time zone, tourists can easily adjust to time variations while hopping between cities.

6. Coordinating International Time Zones:
Comprehending the time zone differences in Medellin is crucial for global visitors, particularly when organizing flights, conferences, or online communications with people around the globe. To guarantee prompt coordination and communication, it is important to take into account the time difference between Medellin and other areas.

In general, knowing the time zone in Medellin—which is Colombian Time (COT) at UTC-5—allows both visitors and residents to efficiently plan their days and activities, guaranteeing seamless transitions between time zones and reducing any possible misunderstanding regarding time differences.

Things to Consider Before Leaving

There are many chances for adventure, cultural immersion, and discovery while visiting Medellin, Colombia. However, before you set off on your voyage, there are a few crucial things to think about. Here's a thorough rundown of important considerations:

1. Visa prerequisites:
- Before visiting Medellin, find out whether you need a visa for your home country. For a limited time, visitors of several nations, including those of the United States, Canada, and the European Union, are permitted entry into Colombia without a visa. To guarantee compliance, it is essential to confirm the most recent visa restrictions.

2. Safety Measures:
Even though Medellin's safety and security have significantly improved recently, it's still important to use care and maintain

vigilance, particularly in certain locations. Minimize the danger of theft or scams by researching the current state of safety, following local safety advice, and avoiding exhibiting precious objects in public.

3. Health-Related Considerations:
Prioritize your health before visiting Medellin by making sure all of your usual shots are current and looking into any vaccinations that may be advised for Colombia. In addition, think about getting travel health insurance to pay for medical costs in the event that you get sick or are injured while traveling. It's a good idea to bring in any necessary prescriptions and, if you have any pre-existing medical issues, to see a doctor.

4. Money and Modes of Payment:
- The Colombian peso (COP) is the country's official currency. Although major credit cards are commonly accepted in Medellin and other cities, smaller purchases, particularly in more isolated locations, are best done using cash. In Medellin, ATMs are well spaced and let you take out local cash as required.

5. Language:
- Medellin and all of Colombia are officially bilingual in Spanish. Even if many people in tourist locations may know a little bit of English, it's still beneficial to learn some fundamental Spanish expressions and phrases to improve communication and your trip. Take into consideration using a pocket-sized phrasebook as a reference or downloading a language app.

6. Weather and Stuffing:

- Medellin has good weather all year round, with typical highs of 15°C to 25°C (59°F to 77°F). Bring a light jacket or sweater for chilly nights and lightweight, breathable attire for warm weather. For outdoor activities, don't forget to pack bug repellant, a hat, sunscreen, and comfortable walking shoes.

7. Customary Conduct:
- Get acquainted with Colombian traditions and cultural standards in order to respect regional practices. Since Colombians are renowned for their friendliness and warmth, extend a warm "Hola" or "Buenos días" to everyone you meet and be willing to strike up a discussion. Steer clear of touchy subjects like drugs or politics, and be aware of how other cultures behave and gesture.

8. Options for Transportation:
- Examine your alternatives for getting about Medellin, such as the effective metro system, taxis, public buses, and ride-sharing services like Uber. To make your way about the city with ease, familiarize yourself with the routes, prices, and safety advice. For day travels outside of Medellin, you could also think about hiring a driver or renting a vehicle for more convenience.

You can guarantee a hassle-free and delightful trip while taking advantage of all that this energetic Colombian city has to offer by taking these things into account before you fly to Medellin.

Transportation Options in Medellin

Because of the effective transit alternatives available in the city, traveling across Medellin as a visitor is not too difficult. This is a thorough tutorial on how to navigate Medellin:

1. Metro:
- Medellin has one of Latin America's most advanced and effective metro systems. The metro's two main lines, Lines A and B, link a number of residential areas and popular tourist destinations. There are handy train stations placed all across the city, and trains operate regularly. The metro is a great way to move about Medellin since it's inexpensive, safe, and clean.

2. Metrocable:
- The Metrocable is an aerial cable car system that is part of the metro system and gives residents access to communities perched on hillsides while also giving breathtaking cityscape vistas. Travelers may use the Metrocable to destinations including Biblioteca España, Parque Arví, and Santo Domingo Savio. It's a distinctive and beautiful approach to discover the many landscapes of Medellin.

3. Metroplus:
- Metroplus is a bus rapid transit network that gives Medellin residents other transportation alternatives in addition to the metro. These contemporary articulated buses move quickly and effectively over longer distances inside the city since they run on dedicated lanes. Travelers may utilize Metroplus to go to places like Laureles, El Poblado, and Envigado that aren't accessible by metro.

4. Buses for the Public:
- There is a vast public bus network in Medellin that links the city's suburbs and communities. Even while buses are sometimes more congested and less pleasant than metro or Metroplus, they are still an affordable way to get throughout Medellin, particularly to places where other forms of

transportation aren't available. Make sure you have correct change or little notes on hand for bus tickets.

5. Taxis:
In Medellin, taxis are easily found and may be booked using ride-hailing applications such as Cabify and Uber, or by hailing one on the street. When there aren't many other choices available, taxis are a practical way to go to certain destinations or get about late at night. Make sure the taximeter is on, or haggle over the fee before you leave.

6. Strolling:
- A lot of Medellin's districts are walkable and ideal for exploring on foot, particularly those in the city center and popular tourist destinations like El Poblado and Laureles. Travelers may enjoy the lively street life of the city, learn about hidden jewels, and fully immerse themselves in the local culture by walking. Just pay attention to pedestrian crossings and cars.

7. Cycle:
- As part of its attempts to encourage cycling as a sustainable form of transportation, Medellin has installed bike lanes and offers rental services in certain locations. Through initiatives like EnCicla, visitors may hire bicycles and take their time exploring Medellin's picturesque parks, riverfronts, and bike-friendly neighborhoods.

Medellin Visa Requirements

Tourists visiting Medellin, Colombia, must have a valid visa depending on their country, the reason for their visit, and how long they want to stay. This is a comprehensive guide to comprehending tourist visa requirements:

1. Entry Without a Visa:
For a limited time, visitors from a number of nations may enter Colombia as tourists without a visa. These nations include the majority of the countries in Latin America, the United States, Canada, member states of the European Union, Australia, and New Zealand. Generally, visitors from nations free from requiring a visa may remain in Colombia for up to 90 days.

2. Arrival visa:
- When arriving at Colombian airports, some nations that are not qualified for visa-free entry may be able to receive a visa on arrival. Certain nations may use this option, therefore visitors should confirm their eligibility and criteria in advance.

3. Extension of Tourist Visa:
- Visitors may apply to the Colombian immigration officials for a tourist visa extension if they want to remain in the country for longer than the original 90 days. With the extension, visitors may remain in the nation for up to 90 more days, for a maximum of 180 days in a calendar year.

4. Procedure for Applying for a Visa:
- To apply for a visa to enter Colombia, visitors from nations where a visa is required must usually submit an application form, passport photos, a valid passport that has at least six months left on it, proof of travel (such as a return ticket),

proof of lodging, and evidence that they have enough money to cover their expenses while in the country.

5. Visa charges:
- Depending on the nationality of the traveller and the kind of visa being requested, there can be costs involved with visa applications. Checking the current visa prices and authorized payment methods at the Colombian consulate or embassy is crucial since rates might differ.

6. Visa Processing Period:
- Depending on the nation and the consulate or embassy where the application is filed, processing times for visa applications differ. It is recommended that travelers give themselves enough time to complete their visa applications, submitting them well in advance of the dates they want to travel.

7. Insurance for Travel:
- While a visa is not necessary, it is strongly advised that visitors to Medellin and Colombia get travel insurance that covers unanticipated situations, medical crises, and trip cancellations. Financial security and peace of mind are offered by travel insurance in the event of crises while traveling.

8. Authorities Consulted:
- For the most recent information on visa requirements, application processes, and other travel-related advisories, travelers should visit the official website of the Colombian Ministry of Foreign Affairs or speak with the closest Colombian consulate or embassy in their home country to ensure compliance with visa requirements and regulations.

Medellin Travel Cost

When organizing a vacation to Medellin, Colombia, one must take into account a number of charges, such as lodging, transportation, food, entertainment, and other incidentals. Here is a thorough explanation of the usual expenses related to a tourist's journey to Medellin:

1. Accommodations:
- Low-cost lodging (guesthouses, hostels): $10 to $30 a night
- Hotels in the midrange: $40 to $100 per night
- Expensive Hotels: Over $100 per night

2. Mode of transportation:
- Each Metro travel costs $0.70.
- Metrocable Ticket: $0.70 for each ride (transfer fees extra)
Metroplus Ticket: $1 for each journey
- $0.70 per journey for a public bus ticket
- Taxi cost: varies based on the distance traveled and the time of day; the beginning cost is often $2.

3. Dinners:
- Snacks and street food: $2 to $5 per meal
- Local eateries (Menu del Día): lunch and supper cost $5 to $10.
- Mid-range Dining: $10 to $20 per course
$20+ per lunch at fine dining establishments

4. Drinks:
- Water in bottles: $0.50 to $1
- $1–$2 soft drinks
- $1 to $2 for local beer (such as Club Colombia or Aguila).
- Drinks: $5 to $10

5. Tasks:
- Museum and gallery entry fees range from $2 to $5.
- $20 to $50 per person for guided excursions (including city, coffee, and hiking trips).
- Outdoor Activities: $20 to $100 per person (zip-lining, trekking, paragliding, etc.)
- Nightlife: $10 to $50 (bar drinks, club cover fee)

6. Other:
- $5 to $10 for a cellphone SIM card (with prepaid credit)
- Gifts & Souvenirs: $5 to $50+
- Gratuities: 10% to 15% of the entire amount paid in restaurants; additional services not included.

7. Insurance for Travel:
The price is based on the age of the passenger, the length of the trip, and the coverage. usually falls between $30 and $100 for a basic coverage.

8. Overall Projected Cost:
- Low-cost Traveler: $30 to $50 daily
- Budget Traveler: $50 to $100 daily
- Luxurious Traveler: Over $100 daily

Remark:
- Prices are an estimate that might change based on location, time of year, and individual preferences.
Travelers should be prepared to haggle over pricing since it's popular in marketplaces and casual situations.
- It's worth asking about discounted pricing for elders or students since certain sights and activities may offer them.
While it may be handy to use credit cards or take out cash from ATMs, keep in mind that there may be costs associated with overseas transactions and currency conversion.

Best Hotels in Medellin for Lodging

Minimum Spending
1. Rango Boutique Hostal:
Address: El Poblado, Calle 10A #42-34
- Approximate Cost: $10 to $20 each night

- Description: In the center of El Poblado, Hostal Rango Boutique provides pleasant individual rooms and dorms at an affordable price. The hostel is perfect for low-cost visitors who want to experience Medellin's exciting nightlife and cultural attractions since it has a rooftop patio, shared kitchen, and social spaces.

2. Hostel Wandering Paisa:
- Address: Laureles, Carrera 36 #8A-36
- Approximate Cost: $10 to $20 each night
- Description: The Wandering Paisa Hostel provides reasonably priced dorm beds and individual rooms in the hip Laureles district. There are frequent social gatherings, group barbecues, and a comfortable common space for guests to enjoy a vibrant environment. The hostel's handy location makes it simple to go to the neighborhood's eateries, pubs, and transit.

3. Hostel Happy Buddha:
- Address: El Poblado, Carrera 35 #7-108
- Approximate Cost: $10 to $20 each night
- Description: Happy Buddha Hostel is a laid-back hostel with affordable lodging in the center of El Poblado. The hostel has a rooftop patio, bar, and community kitchen in addition to private rooms and dorm beds. Visitors may visit neighboring sites including Parque Lleras and Pueblito Paisa thanks to the hotel's strategic location.

4. Hostel Tiger Paw:
- Location: El Poblado, Carrera 41 #9-41
- Approximate Cost: $10 to $20 each night
- Description: Tiger Paw Hostel provides reasonably priced lodging in individual rooms and dorm beds in the bustling El Poblado district. The hostel has many activities, movie nights,

and barbecues, all contributing to its warm and inviting environment. Additionally, visitors may unwind in the garden area outside or explore the neighboring eateries, pubs, and cafés.

Medium Budget:
1. Poblado Plaza Hotel:
- Address: El Poblado, Carrera 43A #4Sur-75
- Approximate Cost: $50 to $100 each night
- Description: Hotel Poblado Plaza provides cozy accommodations with contemporary conveniences in the exclusive El Poblado district. The hotel has an international restaurant, a fitness center, a spa, and an outdoor pool. For mid-range guests looking for comfort and convenience, Hotel Poblado Plaza is well located close to Parque Lleras and retail malls.

2. Hotel Diez, Colombian Category:
- Address: El Poblado, Carrera 43A #1Sur-150
- Approximate Cost: $50 to $100 each night
- Description: Diez Hotel Categoria Colombia, located in the center of El Poblado, provides chic lodging with modern furnishings and first-rate facilities. The hotel has a gourmet restaurant, a fitness facility, a rooftop pool, and roomy suites and rooms. Easy access to neighboring attractions including Museo de Arte Moderno and Parque Lleras is provided to guests.

3. Milla de Oro Hotel Estelar:
- Address: El Poblado, Carrera 43A #3Sur-89
- Approximate Cost: $50 to $100 each night
- Description: Sophisticated lodging with exquisite design and opulent facilities can be found at the Hotel Estelar Milla de Oro, which is situated in El Poblado's famed Milla de Oro

neighborhood. The hotel has a rooftop patio, gourmet restaurant, spa, and roomy suites and rooms. For mid-range guests, Hotel Estelar Milla de Oro offers a sophisticated escape with its convenient location and attentive service.

4. Residence Du Parc Royal:
- Address: El Poblado, Carrera 36 #2Sur-60
- Approximate Cost: $50 to $100 each night
- Description: Located in the peaceful El Poblado district, Hotel Du Parc Royal provides opulent lodging with a French-inspired design and attentive service. The hotel has a fitness facility, rooftop pool, French cuisine, and cozy rooms and suites. Despite being close to El Poblado's services and activities, guests may relax in the hotel's tranquil atmosphere.

Luxurious

1. Hotel Charlie:
- Address: El Poblado, Carrera 37 #8A-97
- Estimated cost per night: $100+
- Description: The Charlee Hotel is a boutique luxury hotel in the center of El Poblado that offers upmarket lodging with cutting-edge technology and contemporary decor. The hotel has a rooftop infinity pool, spa, and gourmet restaurant in addition to its modern rooms and suites. Travelers seeking an opulent experience will find the Charlee Hotel to be very desirable due to its great location and premium services.

2. Park Hotel 10:
- Address: El Poblado, Carrera 36B #11–12.
- Estimated cost per night: $100+
- Description: Situated in the lively El Poblado area, Hotel Park 10 provides tasteful lodging with exquisite furnishings and first-rate service. The hotel has a gourmet restaurant, fitness facility, rooftop terrace, and opulent rooms and suites.

In an elegant atmosphere, guests may take advantage of individualized attention and high-end facilities.

3. NH Collection Royal Medellin:
- Address: El Poblado, Carrera 42 #7-130
- Estimated cost per night: $100+
- Description: The NH Collection Medellin Royal is a luxury hotel with modern decor and expansive city views, tucked away in El Poblado's posh Milla de Oro neighborhood. The hotel has large rooms and suites, a fitness center, a rooftop pool, and a restaurant with a Mediterranean flair. For those seeking an upscale escape, the NH Collection Medellin Royal offers a sophisticated ambience and attentive service.

4. The Intercontinental Hotel Medellin:
- Address: El Poblado, Carrera 1A #16A-06.
- Estimated cost per night: $100+
- Description: Nestled among verdant gardens in El Poblado, the Hotel Intercontinental Medellin provides opulent lodgings accompanied by a tranquil atmosphere and stunning city vistas. The hotel has several dining choices, outdoor pools, tennis courts, spa, and exquisite rooms and suites. This elegant hotel offers unmatched comfort and leisure to its visitors.

Medellin's Finest Restaurant

Minimum Spending

1. John the Old:
- Address: El Centro, Carrera 49 #53-43
- Estimated Cost: $ - $$
- El Viejo John is a well-liked restaurant serving authentic Colombian food at reasonable costs. The menu offers filling items including empanadas, sancocho, and bandeja paisa. Both residents and visitors love the restaurant for its laid-back vibe and welcoming staff.

2. Hacienda Junín:
- Address: El Poblado, Carrera 43F #8-74
- Estimated Cost: $ - $$
Hacienda Junín provides genuine Colombian food in a laid-back atmosphere. The menu highlights the variety of tastes found in Colombian food, with dishes like ajiaco, bandeja paisa, and the delectable arepas and chicharrón. The restaurant is a great option for those on a tight budget because of its reasonable rates and substantial servings.

3. La Fonda Paisa:
- Address: Laureles, Carrera 70 #43-20
- Estimated Cost: $ - $$
- Description: Specializing on authentic Antioquian food, La Fonda Paisa is a delightful restaurant. Classic fare like mondongo, sancocho, and lechona are served to guests in a welcoming setting that is evocative of a rural Colombian farmhouse. Both residents and tourists love the restaurant for its unique tastes and affordable costs.

4. Café Alma y Panadería:
- Address: Laureles, Carrera 73 #43A-51
- Estimated Cost: $ - $$

- Description: Offering freshly made bread, pastries, and Colombian delights, Panadería y Café Al Alma is a pleasant bakery and café. While indulging in mouthwatering arepas, pandebonos, and buñuelos, guests may enjoy fragrant Colombian coffee. The bakery is a great place for breakfast or a quick snack because of its reasonable rates and freshly produced goodies.

Medium Budget
1. Restaurant Carmen:
- Address: El Poblado, Carrera 36 #10A-27
- Estimated Cost: $$ - $$$
- Description: Carmen Restaurante presents creative meals made using ingredients that are found locally, giving a modern take on Colombian cuisine. The menu offers inventive takes on classic dishes including ceviche, grilled meats, and shellfish. The restaurant is a well-liked option for an unforgettable dining experience because of its sophisticated atmosphere and excellent service.

2. The Sky:
- Address: El Poblado, Carrera 40 #10A-22
- Estimated Cost: $$ - $$$
-   El Cielo is a well-known restaurant distinguished by its innovative take on Colombian cuisine. Master chef Juan Manuel Barrientos crafts delectable dishes that arouse the senses and honor Colombia's rich cultural legacy. Taste menus with many courses that showcase creative preparations and inventive cuisine are available for guests to savor.

3. Oci.Mde:
- Address: 8A Calle #37-04, El Poblado
- Estimated Cost: $$ - $$$

- Description: Sophisticated eating at Oci.Mde, with an emphasis on modern cuisine and fresh ingredients. Chef Laura Londoño's creative cuisine, influenced by tastes from throughout the world, are served at the restaurant. In an elegant and exclusive atmosphere, guests may savor delectable culinary masterpieces.

4. Restaurant Haboviejo:
- Address: Laureles, Carrera 73 #C1-62.
- Estimated Cost: $$ - $$$
- Description: Known for its authentic Colombian cuisine served in a quaint colonial-style setting, Hatoviejo Restaurante is a well-liked Medellin institution. There are many different items on the menu, such as succulent stews, grilled meats, and fresh seafood. At this renowned restaurant, visitors may savor a little of the warmth and culinary traditions of Colombia.

Luxurious
1. Mondongo's:
- Location: El Poblado, Carrera 41 #10-9
- Estimated Cost: $$$ - $$$$
- Mondongo's is a posh eatery that specializes in fine Colombian food. The menu offers sophisticated takes on classic recipes made with top-notch ingredients and creative cooking methods. Diners may enjoy delectable tastes and flawless presentations in an opulent setting.

2. Medellín's Sky:
Location: El Poblado, Carrera 38 #8-18
- Estimated Cost: $$$ - $$$$
- Description: El Cielo Medellín showcases Chef Juan Manuel Barrientos' inventive vision and love for gastronomy while providing a gastronomic trip across Colombia's many regions.

The restaurant offers multisensory tasting menus that blend tradition, science, and art to create a truly unique eating experience.

3. Barbara y Cocina Carmen:
Location: El Poblado, Calle 10 #38-38
- Estimated Cost: $$$ - $$$$
- Description: Carmen Cocina y Barra is a modern eatery that honors the culinary traditions of Colombia while incorporating contemporary elements. Chef Carmen Angel creates a polished but genuine culinary experience with her inventive recipes that showcase regional tastes and ingredients.

4. Matrix:
Location: El Poblado, Carrera 35 #8A-6
- Estimated Cost: $$$ - $$$$
- Description: Matria is an elegant dining establishment that emphasizes using products that are produced locally and sustainably. Colombia's gastronomic richness is showcased in every dish by Chef Laura Londoño's creative cuisine, which represents the country's biodiversity and cultural variety. Experience a culinary voyage through the tastes of Colombia in a sophisticated but cozy environment.

Top Medellin Markets And Shopping Centers

Minimum Spending
1. Middle Plaza:
- Location: La Minorista, Carrera 51 #79-140
- Estimated Cost: $ - $$
The main wholesale market in Medellin is called Plaza Minorista, and it provides a huge range of reasonably priced

fresh fruit, meats, seafood, and home items. Discover fantastic discounts on fruits, veggies, and other daily necessities by perusing the busy aisles and chatting with neighborhood merchants.

2. San Alejo Marketplace:
- Address: Carrera 43A, San Antonio, Parque de San Antonio
- Estimated Cost: $ - $$
- Description: Held every Sunday in the San Antonio district, Mercado de San Alejo is a lively flea market. Along with live music and street acts, visitors may peruse booths offering jewelry, apparel, souvenirs, and handcrafted crafts. The market provides a distinctive shopping experience in a vibrant setting.

3. El Rio Marketplace:
- Address: Poblado, Carrera 49B #7Sur-50
- Estimated Cost: $ - $$
In the center of El Poblado lies a chic food hall called Mercado del Rio. Numerous food booths selling foreign fare, such as sushi, pizza, tacos, and Colombian delicacies, can be found at the market. Visitors may enjoy a relaxed eating experience in a vibrant environment while sampling various delicacies.

4. El Hueco:
- Address: 49A Calle, Centro
- Estimated Cost: $ - $$
- Description: Located in Medellin's center, El Hueco, sometimes known as "the hole," is a busy street market. At discounted costs, visitors may purchase a variety of goods, such as apparel, accessories, gadgets, and mementos. Customers should be ready to haggle for the best prices since it's prevalent.

Medium Budget

1. El Tesoro Comercial Centro:
- Address: El Poblado, Carrera 25A #1A Sur-45
- Estimated Cost: $$ - $$$
- Description: With a variety of local and international brands, premium shops, and fine eating choices, Centro Comercial El Tesoro is a top shopping destination in Medellin. The mall is a well-liked location for leisure and shopping because of its contemporary construction, open-air layout, and picturesque vistas.

2. Santa Fe Commercial Center:
- Address: El Poblado, Carrera 43A #7Sur-170
- Estimated Cost: $$ - $$$
One of Medellin's biggest shopping centers, Centro Comercial Santafé is home to a variety of eateries, entertainment venues, retail businesses, and family-friendly activities. After shopping for clothing, gadgets, home products, and other items, visitors may have a bite to eat at one of the mall's several restaurants.

3. Oviedo Commercial Center:
- Address: El Poblado, Carrera 43A #6Sur-15
- Estimated Cost: $$ - $$$
- Description: Located in El Poblado, Centro Comercial Oviedo is a well-known retail mall. The mall offers a wide range of retailers, such as specialized shops, technology stores, and fashion boutiques. A movie theater, food choices, and kid-friendly entertainment are all available to visitors.

4. Envigado Market:
- Address: Envigado, Carrera 43 #38-39
- Estimated Cost: $$ - $$$
The adjacent town of Envigado is home to the historic market known as Mercado de Envigado. Fresh fruit, meats, seafood,

artisanal goods, apparel, accessories, and home goods are all available at the market. The market's booths may be explored by anyone who want to experience the local vibe.

Luxurious

1. Viscaya Commercial Center:
- Address: El Poblado, Carrera 32 #9A-19
- Estimated Cost: $$$ - $$$$
- Description: Known for its elite fashion shops, luxury brands, and exclusive designer stores, Centro Comercial Vizcaya is an upscale shopping mall. The mall attracts wealthy customers looking for elegance and refinement as it offers fine dining establishments, cafés, and entertainment venues.

2. Premium Centro Comercial Plaza:
- Address: El Poblado, Carrera 43A #30-25
- Estimated Cost: $$$ - $$$$
- Description: Showcasing a carefully chosen array of upmarket shops, global brands, and luxury stores, Centro Comercial Premium Plaza provides a first-rate shopping experience. Satisfied customers seeking exclusivity and quality are catered to by the mall's gourmet food selections, smart environment, and attractive design.

3. Santa Fe Centro Comercial:
- Address: El Poblado, Carrera 43A #7Sur-170
- Estimated Cost: $$$ - $$$$
- Centro Comercial Santa Fe is an upmarket department shops, designer boutiques, and prominent brands. It is a center for luxury shopping. Rich customers looking for the best shopping experience in Medellin are drawn to the mall by its posh setting, high-end brands, and VIP services.

4. Oviedo Commercial Center:

- Address: El Poblado, Carrera 43A #6Sur-15
- Estimated Cost: $$$ - $$$$
- Description: Renowned for its upscale stores, luxury brands, and upscale fashion shops, Centro Comercial Oviedo is a popular shopping destination in El Poblado. Rich consumers looking for luxury and sophistication may enjoy exquisite eating selections, expensive facilities, and a sophisticated retail atmosphere at the mall.

CHAPTER 1: MEDELLIN'S TOP CULTURAL ATTRACTIONS

Museo de Antioquia

Location: Medellin, Colombia; Carrera 52 #52-43, Plaza Botero

One of the most significant cultural organizations in Medellin, Colombia, is the Museo de Antioquia. It's situated in Plaza Botero, a busy public plaza named after well-known Colombian artist Fernando Botero, whose enormous sculptures dot the neighborhood. The museum has important pieces by local, regional, and worldwide artists in addition to a vast collection of artworks honoring the rich cultural legacy of the Antioquia area.

Highlights

1. Fernando Botero, one of Colombia's most well-known painters, has a collection of artwork that is the museum's most notable feature. Botero's famous works, which are distinguished by their fanciful style and exaggerated dimensions, are on display for visitors to appreciate.

2. Permanent exhibits: The museum presents a wide variety of permanent exhibits that delve into several topics pertaining to Colombian art, history, and culture, in addition to Botero's creations. Photographs, relics, paintings, and sculptures that shed light on Antioquia's history and present may be found in these shows.

3. Temporary exhibits: The Museo de Antioquia often holds temporary exhibits that focus on social topics, new trends, and contemporary artists. These revolving exhibits provide guests the chance to explore a vibrant and constantly shifting cultural environment.

4. After seeing the museum, tourists may take a leisurely walk around Plaza Botero, where an astonishing collection of Botero's sculptures is on exhibit in the outdoor plaza. For both residents and visitors, the plaza acts as a center of culture and a meeting spot.

Estimated Cost
- General Admission: Between $5 and $10 USD (special exhibits and guided tours may have different rates).
- Seniors and children under 12 enter free of charge with a valid ID.

Important Information for Travelers

- Opening Times: Tuesday through Sunday, 10:00 AM to 6:00 PM, is when the Museo de Antioquia is normally open. When making travel plans, it's best to check the museum's website or get in touch with them directly since they can be closed on Mondays and public holidays.
- Guided Tours: For those who would want to understand more about the artwork and exhibits, the museum provides guided tours in Spanish. whether you can speak English, you may wish to find out whether there are any English-language audio guides or guided tours available.
- Accessibility: The museum has ramps and elevators to make moving around the structure easier for wheelchair users. To guarantee a pleasant visit, visitors with special requirements related to accessibility are asked to get in touch with the museum ahead of time.
- Facilities: The Museo de Antioquia contains a café where guests may buy food and drinks, as well as gift shops and bathrooms.
- Photography: While tripods and flash photography may be prohibited, taking pictures of the museum's permanent exhibits is often permitted. Signage and photography policies should be adhered to by visitors in order to protect the artworks and make sure that everyone has a good time.

The Museo de Antioquia is a must-visit location for travelers looking to fully immerse themselves in Medellin's dynamic cultural scene since it provides an enthralling trip through Colombian art and culture.

Parque Explora

Location: Medellin, Colombia; Carrera 52 #73-75
In the middle of Medellin lies a vibrant scientific museum and interactive center called Parque Explora. Offering a broad variety of educational activities centered on science, technology, and the environment, it is one of the city's top attractions. Visitors of all ages may enjoy an immersive and enjoyable learning experience at Parque Explora thanks to its interactive displays, hands-on exhibits, and interesting activities.

Highlights

1. Interactive exhibitions: Parque Explora offers a broad selection of interactive installations and exhibitions covering astronomy, biology, physics, ecology, and other scientific subjects. In an entertaining and engaging manner, visitors may learn about scientific concepts by doing experiments, participating in presentations, and exploring hands-on exhibits.

2. Aquarium: The museum has a sizable aquarium that displays the variety of aquatic life that may be found in Colombia's lakes, rivers, and seas. Learn about the value of environmental stewardship and marine conservation while taking in the sights of vibrant fish, sharks, turtles, and other aquatic animals in their native environments.

3. Planetarium: The state-of-the-art planetarium at Parque Explora allows guests to go on immersive cosmic adventures. The planetarium provides amazing visual and auditory experiences that take visitors to far-off star systems, galaxies, and celestial events while enlightening them about the glories of the cosmos.

4. Explore the natural world and learn about biodiversity, ecosystems, and sustainability at the museum's Outdoor Exploration Park, which includes a botanical garden, ecological paths, and interactive displays. The park offers a peaceful haven in the middle of the city, perfect for leisure and outdoor activities.

Estimated Cost

General Admission: $10 to $15 USD (prices may change for special events or exhibits).

- Children, elderly, organizations, and students with proper IDs may be eligible for discounted pricing.
- Extra charges might be incurred for unique activities like guided tours or planetarium programs.

Important Information for Travelers
- Opening Times: Tuesday through Sunday from 9:00 AM to 5:30 PM is when Parque Explora is normally open. Prior to making travel plans, tourists should check the museum's website or get in touch with them directly since they may be closed on Mondays and other holidays.
- Guided Tours: For those who want to examine the exhibits and learn from knowledgeable experts, the museum provides guided tours in Spanish. whether you can speak English, you may wish to find out whether there are any English-language audio guides or guided tours available.
- Accessibility: Parque Explora has ramps, elevators, and parking places reserved for those with impairments. It is also wheelchair accessible. The museum gives help upon request and works to make sure that every visitor has an inclusive experience.
- Facilities: The museum provides coffee shops, bathrooms, and gift stores where visitors may buy informational and souvenir items. In addition, there are outdoor dining and lounging spaces with picnic tables.

With its engaging combination of education and fun, Parque Explora is a favorite hangout for scientific enthusiasts, school groups, and families. Visitors to Parque Explora are certain to have an amazing and fascinating experience, whether they want to perform experiments in the interactive displays, marvel at marine life in the aquarium, or explore the wonders of the cosmos in the planetarium.

Comuna 13 Tour de Graffiti

Address: 13 Comuna Medellin, Colombia

Visitors get a rare chance to see one of Medellin's liveliest and most culturally important districts with the Comuna 13 Graffiti Tour. Once notorious for its high rates of crime and violence, Comuna 13 has seen a dramatic change in recent years, partly because of community projects and street art. It is now renowned for its vibrant murals, motivational street art, and strong character.

Highlights

1. Street Art Murals: As the trip winds through Comuna 13's narrow lanes, guests may take in an amazing array of graffiti murals and street art made by both domestic and foreign artists. The murals cover a broad spectrum of subjects, including cultural heritage, communal pride, human rights, and social justice.

2. Historical Narratives: Skillful guides narrate Comuna 13's history and development throughout the trip, offering insights into the neighborhood's turbulent past and its path toward peace and reconciliation. Visitors discover the community's inventiveness, resiliency, and will to triumph despite hardship.

3. The chance to ride the outdoor escalators, which were erected as part of an urban development initiative to enhance accessibility and mobility in the area, is one of the tour's highlights. With their expansive views of Comuna 13 and the slopes around it, the escalators give a unique viewpoint on the area's change.

4. Community involvement: The tour places a strong emphasis on community empowerment and involvement, showcasing the part played by locals in reviving Comuna 13 via social projects, art, and culture. Visitors may engage in conversation with locals, show support for area businesses, and discover what ongoing initiatives are being done to enhance the neighborhood's standard of living.

Estimated Cost
- Tour costs vary based on the tour operator, length of trip, and included items.

The average cost of a guided group tour is between $10 and $30 USD per person.
- Customized experiences or private excursions could be more expensive.
- Some trips could include with extra activities, food, or transportation.

Important Information for Travelers
- Reservations: To guarantee your seat on the Comuna 13 Graffiti Tour, it is advised that you make reservations in advance with a respectable tour operator or guide. Numerous tour alternatives are available for visitors to choose from, such as personalized excursions catered to their interests and preferences, walking tours, and bike tours.
- Safety: Although Comuna 13 has significantly improved security and safety, visitors should always use care and adhere to local laws. It's best to go on guided excursions with experienced guides who know the region well and can guarantee a fun and safe experience.
- Comfortable Attire: Put on stroller- and outdoor exploration-friendly attire and sneakers. Participants should be ready for moderate physical exercise since the tour may include some walking and stairs.
- Photography: While taking pictures of the trip is welcomed, guests are asked to respect the privacy of the inhabitants and get permission before shooting images of people or private property. Remember to bring your camera or smartphone since there are plenty of murals and artworks that provide excellent picture possibilities.
- Support Local Businesses: During the tour, stop at small shops or street vendors to buy beverages, snacks, or souvenirs in order to show your support for the businesses in your community. Your donations support community-based activities and aid in the economic growth of the area.

Visitors interested in learning more about Medellin's creative expression, social change, and cultural legacy will find the Comuna 13 Graffiti Tour to be a fascinating and rewarding experience.

Jardín Botánico de Medellín

Location: Medellin, Colombia; Calle 73 #51D-14

The luxuriant Medellin Botanical Garden, also known as the Jardín Botánico de Medellín, lies close to the city's center. The botanical garden, which covers an area of more than 14 hectares, is home to a wide variety of plant species from Colombia and other countries. It provides chances for leisure, learning, and taking in the beauty of nature, making it a tranquil haven for both residents and visitors.

Highlights

1. Botanical Collections: There are many different types of plants in the garden, such as species from the tropical rainforest, native Colombian plants, bromeliads, orchids, palm trees, and succulents. Explore themed gardens that highlight the variety and complexity of Colombia's ecosystems, such as the Aquatic Garden, Arid Garden, and Orchid Garden.

2. Butterfly Sanctuary: The Butterfly Sanctuary, also known as the Mariposario, is one of the garden's primary draws. Here, guests may see vibrant butterflies in their native environment. The sanctuary's luxuriant flora, water features, and feeding stations are all intended to draw in and sustain a healthy population of butterflies.

3. Programs for Education: The Jardín Botánico provides guided tours and educational activities for guests of all ages,

including families, school groups, and nature lovers. Offering insightful information on Colombia's botanical legacy, knowledgeable interpreters give tours that highlight the garden's plant collections, ecological significance, and conservation initiatives.

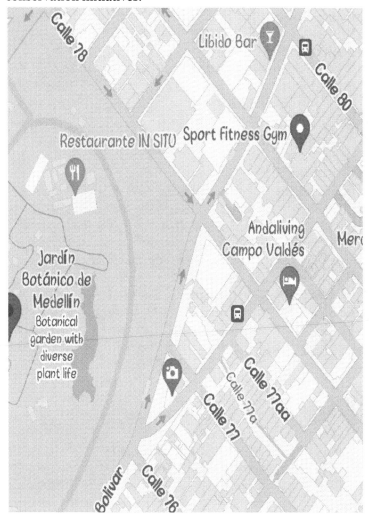

4. Cultural Events: The botanical garden holds seminars, exhibits, and cultural events all year long that honor the arts, music, literature, and environmental sustainability. To enhance their visit and interaction with the garden, visitors may take part in events including yoga sessions, art exhibits, outdoor concerts, and gardening seminars.

Estimated Cost
- General Admission: $2 to $5 USD per person (prices may change for exhibits or special events).
- Seniors and children under 12 enter free of charge with a valid ID.
- Workshops, unique experiences, and guided excursions may incur additional costs.

Important Information for Travelers
- Opening Times: Tuesday through Sunday from 9:00 AM to 4:30 PM is when the Jardín Botánico de Medellin is normally open. Prior to making travel plans, guests should check the garden's website or get in touch with them personally since it can be closed on Mondays and other holidays.
- Accessibility: The garden has ramps, paved paths, and parking places reserved for those with impairments, making it wheelchair accessible. The garden gives help upon request and works to make sure that every visitor has an inclusive experience.
- Facilities: There are picnic spaces, bathrooms, and a café where guests may buy food and beverages in the botanical garden. Additionally, there are gift stores offering literature, souvenirs, and plant-related goods.
- Photography: Personal use of photography is allowed in the garden's outdoor spaces, but commercial use of photography or filmmaking may need permission in advance. To safeguard the plant collections and maintain the garden's natural

beauty, visitors should abide by any signs or photographic restrictions.

Nestled within lush vegetation, the Jardín Botánico de Medellin invites tourists to discover botanical marvels, reconnect with nature, and enjoy cultural events in a serene haven from the bustle of the city. Wandering through themed gardens, watching butterflies fly, or going to a cultural event—guests to this urban paradise are certain to come away inspired and feeling refreshed.

Plaza Botero

Address: 52 Carrera Medellin, Colombia

Located in the center of Medellin, Plaza Botero is a lively public space that bears the name of the well-known Colombian artist Fernando Botero. The plaza is well-known for its collection of enormous sculptures by Botero, a prominent artist whose unique style is characterized by exaggerated dimensions and quirky shapes. Admire these famous pieces of art, meander about the outdoor plaza, and take in the lively vibe of one of Medellin's most well-known attractions as you visit Plaza Botero.

Highlights

1. Botero Sculptures: The greatest collection of Fernando Botero's works in a public area, Plaza Botero is home to 23 bronze sculptures that the artist himself contributed. Botero's distinct style and sense of humor are evident in the sculptures, which portray a diverse range of topics such as animals, human figures, and commonplace things.

2. Open-Air Museum: Plaza Botero is an outdoor museum where guests are welcome to tour the neighborhood at their

own pace and have free access to Botero's sculptures. The plaza is a great place to unwind, people-watch, and immerse yourself in the local culture because of its central position, shaded sitting spaces, and pedestrian-friendly design.

3. Cultural Landmark: In addition to its artistic value, Plaza Botero is a symbol of Medellin's dedication to public art and

rehabilitation, as well as the city's changing urban environment. The plaza is a popular destination for visitors, residents, artists, and photographers. It provides a lively setting for events, celebrations, and social meetings.

Estimated Cost
- There is no charge for anybody to enter Plaza Botero.
- Additional costs might include getting to and from the plaza, buying food or drinks from surrounding merchants, or purchasing mementos from street sellers offering crafts and artwork.

Important Information for Travelers
- Location: Plaza Botero is conveniently situated in the heart of Medellin's center, making it easy to get there on foot, via taxi, or by public transit. The plaza, which is close to other attractions including the Museo de Antioquia and Parque Berrio, may be found with a GPS or map.
- Timing: There are no specific hours for the plaza; it is accessible to the public all year round. While Plaza Botero is open to visitors at all times of the day, it is usually busiest in the afternoon when both residents and visitors assemble to take in the atmosphere and appreciate the sculptures.
- Safety: Although Plaza Botero is usually seen to be safe for tourists, it's still a good idea to use care and pay attention to your possessions, particularly in busy places. Travelers should be mindful of their surroundings and refrain from flashing their valuables or bringing a lot of cash with them.
- Photography: Visitors are free to snap pictures of the sculptures and the surrounding area for their own personal use, and photography is welcomed in Plaza Botero. Posing with the statues and taking unposed pictures of street entertainers and merchants are popular pastimes for tourists.

- Local Amenities: Restrooms, cafés, and street sellers offering refreshments, beverages, and mementos are all located around the plaza. While touring Plaza Botero, visitors may make use of these amenities and show support for neighborhood businesses.

With its charming fusion of art, culture, and community, Plaza Botero invites guests to interact with the recognizable sculptures of Fernando Botero and take in the liveliness of Medellin's cityscape. When visiting Plaza Botero in Medellin, visitors are likely to find it to be a wonderful and rewarding experience, whether they are there to take in the artwork, mingle with the locals, or just enjoy the atmosphere.

CHAPTER 2: NATURAL ATTRACTIONS OF MEDELLÍN

Parque Arví

Location: Santa Elena, Colombia's Medellin
Situated just outside of Medellin, Parque Arví is a vast natural reserve that provides tourists with a picturesque getaway into the natural world. The park, which spans more than 16,000 hectares of protected area, is home to a wide variety of species, lush woods, and clear streams. It is a refuge for biodiversity. Hikers, birdwatchers, outdoor enthusiasts, and anybody interested in seeing Medellin's natural marvels and natural beauty will find Parque Arví to be a popular site.

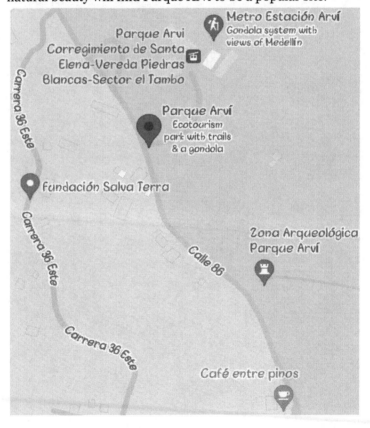

Highlights

1. Pathways for Ecology: Parque Arví is home to a network of ecological paths that meander across the park's many habitats, including as montane forests, cloud forests, and páramo settings. Hikers may follow designated trails and find secret waterfalls, interesting wildlife, and picturesque vistas.

2. Environmental Education: To promote knowledge of environmental preservation and sustainable living, the park provides educational programs and informative displays. Through interactive exhibits, seminars, and guided tours, visitors may learn about the local indigenous cultures, the necessity of biodiversity protection, and the ecological significance of the park.

3. Outdoor Recreation: There are several outdoor recreational activities available at Parque Arví, including as hiking, mountain biking, horseback riding, and camping. With a vast network of trails that appeal to hikers of all experience levels, the park has enough to offer everyone, from easy nature hikes to strenuous mountain climbs.

4. Cultural activities: Parque Arví provides cultural activities that highlight the region's rich legacy and customs, in addition to its natural charms. Visitors may immerse themselves in the cultural fabric of the neighboring villages of Medellin by taking part in indigenous rites, traditional craft activities, and gourmet tastes.

Estimated Cost
- A day ticket or admission charge is usually needed to enter Parque Arví; the cost varies according on the activities and amenities available inside the park.

Workshops, guided tours, and unique experiences might cost extra.
- Costs for meals, beverages, and any equipment rentals or transportation to and from the park should be included into the budget of visitors.

Important Information for Travelers
- How to Get There: Parque Arví can be reached via taxi, public transit, or private automobile from Medellin's center in about thirty minutes. Travelers may take the metro to the Acevedo station, where they can change to the Arví Cable Car. The ride offers picturesque vistas as it climbs to the Santa Elena park entrance.

- Park Amenities: Parque Arví features facilities like picnic sites, bathrooms, visitor centers, and food stands where guests may buy snacks and drinks. For those who want to spend the night in the park, there are also dedicated camping spots and hotel choices.

- Safety Measures: When visiting Parque Arví, guests should stick to designated pathways, bring enough water and supplies, and exercise care when around animals and inclement weather. Using sunscreen and insect repellent, dressing in layers, wearing supportive footwear, and protecting yourself from the heat and biting insects are all recommended.

- Guided Tours: To improve their experience, guests might think about taking a guided tour or hiring a local guide, who may provide knowledge about the ecology, history, and cultural value of the park. There are alternatives for private parties and bespoke itineraries, and guided excursions are offered in both Spanish and English.

- Environmental Conservation: To lessen their influence on the park's delicate ecosystems, visitors are urged to follow the Leave No Trace philosophy. This entails tidying up after yourself, keeping animals at bay, and abiding by park laws and regulations.

Offering a peaceful haven from Medellin's busy city life, Parque Arví beckons guests to rediscover the natural world, investigate ecological marvels, and get fully immersed in the highlands of Colombia's rich cultural legacy. Parque Arví is a gratifying and refreshing location for travelers visiting Medellin, whether they want to hike through virgin woods, learn about sustainable living, or just enjoy the pure mountain air.

Piedra del Peñol

El Peñol Rock, or Piedra del Peñol, is a large granite rock formation close to the town of Guatapé, about two hours' drive from Medellin. The rock, which rises 200 meters above the surroundings, provides sweeping views of Antioquia's verdant farmland and the scenic Guatapé Reservoir. A well-liked day excursion from Medellin is to Piedra del Peñol, which draws travelers and nature lovers looking for breathtaking views and exhilarating adventures.

Highlights
1. Climb to the Top: Piedra del Peñol's greatest draw is the chance to ascend the 740 stairs to the rock's top, which provides breath-taking vistas of the surrounding reservoir and landscape. For tourists of all ages, the climb might be difficult but is rewarding at the summit with breathtaking panoramic views, creating an unforgettable experience.

2. Views of the Guatapé Reservoir, a man-made lake filled with hundreds of little islands and peninsulas, are breathtaking from the top of Piedra del Peñol. The emerald-green waters of the reservoir provide a striking contrast to the colorful settlements and lush slopes, making it an ideal setting for memories and photographs.

3. Guatapé Town: Following their descent from Piedra del Peñol, tourists may stroll through this quaint town, which is well-known for its brilliant murals and brightly colored streets

and homes. The town is a fun spot to stroll, buy for trinkets, and enjoy the local cuisine because of its vibrant ambiance, artisan stores, and waterfront promenade.

4. Outdoor Activities: Boat trips, kayaking, zip-lining, and hiking are just a few of the outdoor activities available to tourists to the region besides climbing Piedra del Peñol. In addition to providing chances for swimming, fishing, and water sports, the Guatapé Reservoir's surrounding landscape is perfect for birding and nature excursions.

Estimated Cost
- The cost of admission to climb Piedra del Peñol is between $5 and $10 USD per person.
- Optional costs might include boat rentals, guided excursions, lunches and snacks bought in town, and transportation to and from Guatapé.
- Children, elders, organizations, and students with proper IDs may be eligible for discounts.

Important Information for Travelers
- How to Get There: Piedra del Peñol is about two hours from Medellin by bus or automobile, close to the town of Guatapé. From Medellin's Terminal del Norte, tourists may take the bus to Guatapé, from whence they can take a cab or tuk-tuk to the rock. From Medellin, a few travel companies also provide guided day excursions to Piedra del Peñol.
- Climbing Advice: Since Piedra del Peñol is a physically challenging climb, guests should pack a lot of water and wear comfortable shoes. Climbers may take a breather and take in the scenery at several rest spots spaced throughout the stairway. Starting the ascent early in the day is also advised to avoid crowds and hot weather.

- Safety Measures: Although scaling Piedra del Peñol is normally safe, visitors should proceed with care and follow the safety instructions posted at the location. On the steep stairs, watch your footing and take rests as necessary. Steer clear of climbing in bad weather or if you have health issues that might be made worse by physical activity.
- Exploring Guatapé: Following their visit to Piedra del Peñol, tourists may spend time seeing Guatapé, a town renowned for its vivid architecture and lively culture. Make sure to visit the neighborhood market, take a leisurely walk along the waterfront promenade, and indulge in some classic Colombian food like empanadas and arepas.
- Photography: To fully appreciate the breathtaking views from the peak, remember to include a camera or smartphone. Piedra del Peñol provides plenty of picture chances. Remember to take some pictures to remember your visit to the rock because of its distinctive geological characteristics and expansive views.

Piedra del Peñol is a must-visit location for those visiting the Medellin region since it provides an exhilarating journey and breathtaking natural beauty. Experience Piedra del Peñol like never before, whether it's strolling around Guatapé's vibrant streets, hiking to the mountain for expansive vistas, or engaging in outdoor sports on the reservoir.

Parque Regional Natural El Salado

Location: Envigado, Colombia, close to Medellin
Situated not far from Medellin in the municipality of Envigado, Parque Regional Natural El Salado is a peaceful natural reserve. With lush woods, pure streams, and a variety of animal habitats, the park, which spans more than 165 hectares of protected property, provides visitors with a

tranquil haven in the middle of nature. El Salado offers chances for outdoor leisure and ecological exploration and is a well-liked location for hiking, birding, picnics, and nature photography.

Highlights

1. Hiking paths: El Salado is home to a system of clearly designated hiking paths that run through the park's many ecosystems, which include habitats found in grasslands, riparian zones, and cloud forests. There are many different path choices available to visitors, ranging from casual nature walks to strenuous hikes. Each trail offers a different viewpoint on the park's biodiversity and natural beauty.

2. Biodiversity: A wide variety of plant and animal species, including as native trees, orchids, butterflies, birds, and small animals, may be found in the park. Discovering vibrant bird species like tanagers, hummingbirds, and toucans will excite birdwatchers, and nature lovers will be astounded by the variety of plants and animals that can be discovered within the park's limits.

3. El Salado has dedicated picnic spaces and rest breaks so that guests may relax, eat, and take in the peaceful atmosphere of the park. With picnic tables, chairs, and barbeque grills available, it's the perfect place for families, friends, and lone travelers to get together and relax in the great outdoors.

4. Environmental Education: To promote knowledge of environmental preservation and sustainable living, the park provides educational programs and informative displays. Through guided tours, seminars, and interactive exhibits, visitors may learn about the local flora and wildlife, conservation efforts, and the ecological significance of the park.

Estimated Cost
- The cost of admission to El Salado Regional Natural Park is between $2 and $5 USD per person.

- There can be extra costs for certain classes, special events, and guided tours.
- Costs for meals, beverages, and any equipment rentals or transportation to and from the park should be included into the budget of visitors.

Important Information for Travelers
- How to Get There: The Parque Regional Natural El Salado is situated near Envigado, not far from the heart of Medellin. The park is accessible to visitors by taxi, public transit, or private automobile. For those who are driving their own cars, there is parking close to the park entrance.

- Park Amenities: El Salado has facilities like bathrooms, picnic spaces, visitor centers, and nature paths with interpretive signs and signage. Additionally, there are designated lookout towers and observation sites where guests may take in expansive views of the surroundings.

- Safety Advice: When visiting El Salado, tourists should stick to designated routes, refrain from upsetting animals, and pack for inclement weather. To guard against sun exposure and bug bites, it's advised to wear sturdy footwear, bring enough water and snacks, and use sunscreen and insect repellent.

- Guided Tours: For a more enriching experience, guests could think about going on one of the informative tours conducted by park rangers or local guides. Visitors may learn more about the park's history, ecology, and conservation initiatives by taking one of the guided tours, which help them develop a greater appreciation for nature.

- Photography: With its picturesque landscapes, varied ecosystems, and profusion of species, El Salado provides a wealth of chances for nature photography. It is recommended that guests pack a camera or smartphone to record their trip and capture the splendor of the park's flora and fauna.

For those looking to get away from the bustle of the city and re-establish a connection with nature, Parque Regional Natural El Salado provides a tranquil haven and an immersive natural experience. When visiting El Salado in Medellin, visitors may discover inspiration and peace whether they're trekking through beautiful woods, birding along serene streams, or having a picnic among lush foliage.

Cerro Nutibara

Highlights

Cerro Nutibara is a prominent hill located in the heart of Medellin, offering breathtaking panoramic views of the cityscape below. Here are some highlights of Cerro Nutibara:

1. Mirador: At the summit of Cerro Nutibara, visitors can enjoy panoramic views of Medellin and its surrounding

mountains. The viewpoint provides an excellent vantage point for capturing stunning photographs of the city skyline.

2. Pueblito Paisa: One of the main attractions on Cerro Nutibara is Pueblito Paisa, a replica of a traditional Colombian village. Visitors can explore the charming streets lined with colorful colonial-style buildings, browse local handicrafts at the artisan market, and sample traditional Colombian cuisine at the onsite restaurants.

3. Botanical Garden: Cerro Nutibara is also home to a botanical garden featuring a diverse collection of native plants and flowers. Visitors can stroll along winding pathways, admire exotic flora, and relax in peaceful green spaces surrounded by nature.

4. Cultural Exhibits: Throughout Cerro Nutibara, visitors will find cultural exhibits and educational displays highlighting the history and heritage of Medellin and its people. From historical artifacts to contemporary art installations, there's plenty to discover on the hillside.

Cost Estimate
- Entrance to Cerro Nutibara is typically free of charge, allowing visitors to explore the hill and its attractions at no cost.
- However, there may be optional fees for certain activities or attractions within Cerro Nutibara, such as guided tours of Pueblito Paisa or special exhibitions at the botanical garden.
- Visitors should budget for any additional expenses, such as transportation to and from Cerro Nutibara, souvenirs, and refreshments.

Useful Information for Tourists

- Location: Cerro Nutibara is located in the center of Medellin, easily accessible by public transportation or taxi.
- Operating Hours: The hill is typically open to visitors during daylight hours, but specific hours may vary for attractions such as Pueblito Paisa and the botanical garden.
- Accessibility: While Cerro Nutibara offers stunning views and cultural attractions, visitors should be prepared for steep inclines and uneven terrain, especially when hiking to the summit.
- Safety: Visitors are advised to take precautions against sun exposure and stay hydrated, especially during hot weather. It's also recommended to secure belongings and be aware of surroundings while exploring Cerro Nutibara.

Cerro Nutibara is a must-visit destination for tourists seeking panoramic views, cultural experiences, and natural beauty in the heart of Medellin. Whether you're admiring the city skyline from the mirador, exploring the charming streets of Pueblito Paisa, or immersing yourself in the tranquility of the botanical garden, Cerro Nutibara offers something for every traveler to enjoy.

CHAPTER 3: BEACHES AND WATER SPORTS

Playa El Salado

Location: Envigado, Colombia, close to Medellin

A short distance from Medellin, in the Envigado district, lies an artificial beach park called Playa El Salado. With its sandy beaches, swimming pools, and recreational amenities for guests of all ages, the park—which is tucked away within lush vegetation—offers a cool respite from the heat of the city. Families, parties, and travelers looking for fun, sun, and relaxation in a tropical environment often go to Playa El Salado.

Highlights

1. Artificial Beach: With smooth sand, palm trees, and umbrellas, Playa El Salado's expansive artificial beach area creates a tropical atmosphere evocative of a seaside resort. Guests may enjoy views of the surrounding mountains while lounging on the beach, making sandcastles, or just soaking up the sun.

2. Swimming Pools: The park has a number of pools of different dimensions and depths, including a large main pool and smaller kid-only wading areas. For guests of all ages, the pools' water features, slides, and splash zones provide unlimited entertainment and aquatic pleasure.

3. Recreational facilities: Playa El Salado has a variety of recreational facilities and activities in addition to its beach and pools. Sports fields for soccer or volleyball, kid-friendly playgrounds, covered picnic places with grills, and trails for leisurely walks in the outdoors are a few examples of these.

4. Scenery: Nestled among verdant foliage and scenic vistas, Playa El Salado provides a peaceful haven away from Medellin's hustle and bustle. The park's lovely surroundings—gardens, trees, and flowers—create a calm environment perfect for leisure activities and relaxation.

Estimated Cost
- The cost of an entry ticket or day pass to enter Playa El Salado normally varies according on the time of year, the day of the week, and the kind of visitor (e.g., adult, kid, senior).
- Renting patio chairs or umbrellas, taking part in sports competitions or guided activities, or buying food, beverages, or snacks from on-site vendors may all incur optional costs.

Important Information for Travelers
- Operating Hours: Playa El Salado is normally open everyday throughout the day, however there may be seasonal variations or operating hours that are affected by maintenance or special events. When making travel plans, it's best to check the park's website or get in touch with them directly to find out the current hours of operation.

- transit: Taxis, private vehicles, and public transit may all be used to get to Playa El Salado. For those coming by automobile, the park may provide on-site parking; entrance costs must be paid in advance.

- Facilities: For the comfort of guests, Playa El Salado offers services including showers, changing rooms, and bathrooms. Within the park, there could also be snack bars, cafés, or food sellers offering light fare and drinks.

- Safety: Although Playa El Salado is a kid-friendly and secure location, guests should use care around water and follow any written safety instructions. While there may be lifeguards on duty in designated swimming sites, it is still advisable for parents to watch over their children, particularly if they are little or novice swimmers.

- Accessibility: The park makes an effort to provide wheelchair-accessible spaces, ramps, and paved walkways for guests of all ages and abilities. When they arrive, guests with specific requirements or mobility issues may ask about accommodations or help.

In the center of Medellin, Playa El Salado provides a tropical haven where guests are welcome to unwind, rest, and have fun in the water among verdant surroundings. Vacationers will undoubtedly find Playa El Salado to be a beautiful location for leisure and pleasure, whether they want to explore the recreational activities, splash about in the pools, or lounge on the beach.

Aeroparque Juan Pablo II

Location: Colombia's Medellin

Medellin's Aeroparque Juan Pablo II, sometimes referred to as Aeroparque, is a recreational park next to Olaya Herrera Airport. Aeroparque is a well-liked hangout for families, residents, and visitors looking for outdoor fun and leisure even though it's not a real airport. The park offers a tropical haven in the middle of the city with its wide artificial beach area, swimming pools, green areas, and recreational amenities.

Highlights

1. Artificial Beach: With sand, palm trees, and lounge chairs, Aeroparque's artificial beach area is its focal point. Sunbathing, picnics, and relaxing are popular activities at the beach as it gives visitors the feeling of being at the beach without having to leave the city.

2. Swimming Pools: Aeroparque accommodates guests of all ages and swimming skills with a number of swimming pools that vary in size and depth. The pools provide great aquatic fun for everybody, whether you're wanting to cool down on a hot day, swim laps, or just splash about with the family.

3. Recreational attractions: Aeroparque offers a variety of recreational attractions in addition to the beach and swimming pools. These might include basketball or volleyball courts, kid-friendly playgrounds, picnic spaces with grills, and covered pavilions for lounging.

4. Scenery: Aeroparque is surrounded by rich flora and gives views of the surrounding mountains and city skyline, even though it is close to the airport. The park is a delightful diversion from the bustle of the city because of its quiet ambience and tropical vegetation.

Estimated Cost
- Visitors to Aeroparque Juan Pablo II often pay no admission fee.
- There may be additional costs associated with some park features and activities, such as sports equipment or lounge chair rentals.
- The cost of transportation to and from Aeroparque, as well as any food, beverages, or snacks bought at the park, should be included in.

Important Information for Travelers
- Operating Hours: Depending on the day of the week and season, Aeroparque Juan Pablo II is usually open everyday from the morning until the early evening. It's a good idea to confirm the park's hours of operation before making travel arrangements.

- Parking: If guests are coming by vehicle or motorbike, the park may provide on-site parking. If there are parking costs, they must be paid upon entering the park.
- Facilities: For the comfort of its guests, Aeroparque offers services including showers, changing rooms, and bathrooms. Within the park, there could also be snack bars or food sellers offering beverages.
- Safety: Although Aeroparque is a family-friendly and safe place to visit, guests should still use common sense to make sure they have a good time. This include keeping an eye on kids near water, using sunscreen, drinking enough of water, and locking up valuables to keep them safe from loss or theft.
- Accessibility: With paved walkways, ramps, and spaces reserved for wheelchair users, Aeroparque Juan Pablo II is accessible to guests of all ages and abilities. The park works to provide a welcoming atmosphere where people of all backgrounds may engage in leisure activities and outdoor recreation.

In the center of Medellin, Aeroparque Juan Pablo II provides a distinctive fusion of outdoor activities, water enjoyment, and seaside leisure. Aeroparque is a great place for tourists to relax and have fun, whether they're taking a bath in the pools, having a picnic with loved ones, or just relaxing on the beach.

Aquamundo

Location: Colombia's Rionegro, close to Medellin
A short distance from Medellin, in the municipality of Rionegro, lies the well-known water park known as Aquamundo. The park, which is surrounded by beautiful scenery and lush vegetation, is a popular hangout for thrill-seekers, families, and parties seeking fun and

excitement in a tropical environment. It also provides a range of water activities and recreational amenities.

Highlights

1. Water Attractions: With a large selection of water slides and attractions, Aquamundo can accommodate guests of all ages and tastes. The park provides an abundance of aquatic activities, including wave pools, lazy rivers, and exhilarating water slides.

2. Wave Pool: One of Aquamundo's primary attractions is its large wave pool, where guests may lay and relax in the water or surf mild waves. A cool respite from the summer heat is offered by the wave pool, which simulates a beach with palm palms and sandy shoreline.

3. Adventure Zones: Pirate ships, water cannons, and interactive fountains are just a few of the kid-friendly play areas and themed adventure zones that Aquamundo has to offer. These spaces are meant to encourage kids' imaginations and creativity while providing a secure, watched-over setting for them to splash about in.

4. Relaxation spaces: Aquamundo has dedicated relaxation spaces and lounging locations where guests may rest and soak up the sun in addition to its action-packed activities. The park offers many of places to relax and rejuvenate, whether it's by the pool with a massage, sunbathing, or relaxing in a cabana.

Estimated Cost

- To enter Aquamundo, one must normally buy an admission ticket or day pass, the cost of which varies according on the visitor's age, the day of the week, and the season.

- There may be extra charges for certain park experiences or attractions, such as cabana rentals, workshops, and guided activities.
- The cost of transportation to and from Aquamundo, as well as any food, beverages, or snacks bought at the park, should be included in.

Important Information for Travelers
- Operating Hours: During the warmer months, Aquamundo is normally open every day from early in the morning until late afternoon or early evening. It is best to visit the park's website or get in touch with them directly to find out about any upcoming events or promotions as well as the current operating hours.

- transit: There is enough of on-site parking for guests driving their own automobiles, and visitors may arrive at Aquamundo via taxi, public transit, or private vehicle. Additionally, certain travel companies could provide organized day tours from Medellin to the park.

- Facilities: For the comfort of its guests, Aquamundo offers services including showers, changing rooms, and bathrooms. Additionally, there are cafés, restaurants, and snack bars offering a range of foods and drinks, from light snacks to substantial dinners.

- Safety: Although guest happiness and safety are Aquamundo's top priorities, guests should abide by the established rules and regulations, particularly when using the water slides or engaging in other water-based activities. Throughout the park, lifeguards are positioned to keep an eye on the swimming areas and provide aid as required.

- Accessibility: The park makes an effort to provide wheelchair-accessible spaces, ramps, and paved walkways for guests of all ages and abilities. When they arrive, guests with specific requirements or mobility issues may ask about accommodations or help.

With its exhilarating and revitalizing retreat from the city, Aquamundo welcomes visitors to spend a day of aquatic adventure and enjoyment in the breathtaking natural surroundings. Whether cruising down rapid water slides, surfing in the wave pool, or just lounging by the pool, guests visiting Aquamundo will undoubtedly create treasured moments while visiting Medellin.

Parque Norte

Location: Colombia's Medellin
Popular recreational park Parque Norte is situated in Medellin and provides a range of leisure activities and attractions for guests of all ages. With its water slides, sports facilities, and swimming pools, Parque Norte offers a cool and enjoyable diversion from the bustle of the city. For anyone looking for family-friendly entertainment, aquatic experiences, or just a place to decompress, Parque Norte offers much to offer.

Highlights
1. Water Attractions: To help guests cool down and have fun in the water, Parque Norte offers a variety of swimming pools, water slides, and splash zones. There are water activities at the park for all ages and tastes, from mild pools for leisure to exhilarating slides for thrill-seekers.

2. Lazy River: Nestled between verdant foliage and picturesque vistas, Parque Norte has a lazy river that invites

tourists to stroll idly along a meandering canal. The park's natural beauty may be appreciated by tourists while they unwind and enjoy a refreshing and soothing experience at the lazy river.

3. Play structures, small pools geared at younger guests, and interactive water elements can all be found in Parque Norte's dedicated children's section. Families with kids love it since it's a secure, supervised place for them to splash, slide, and explore.

4. Sports Facilities: Parque Norte has volleyball courts, soccer fields, and basketball courts for guests to enjoy leisure activities and friendly games in addition to its aquatic attractions. The park offers chances for exercise and collaboration while promoting outdoor pleasure and physical wellness.

Estimated Cost
- To enter Parque Norte, one must normally buy an admission ticket or day pass, the cost of which varies based on the visitor's age, the day of the week, and the season.
- There may be extra charges for some park experiences or attractions, such as locker rentals, workshops, and guided activities.
- In addition to any food, beverages, or snacks they may buy at the park, visitors should include in the cost of transportation to and from Parque Norte.

Important Information for Travelers
- Operating Hours: During the warmer months, Parque Norte is normally open everyday from early in the morning until late afternoon or early evening. It is best to visit the park's website or get in touch with them directly to find out about any

upcoming events or promotions as well as the current operating hours.

- transit: There is on-site parking for people driving their own automobiles, and visitors may arrive at Parque Norte by taxi, public transit, or private vehicle. Additionally, certain travel companies could provide organized day tours from Medellin to the park.

- Facilities: For the comfort of its guests, Parque Norte offers services including showers, bathrooms, and changing areas. Additionally, there are cafés, restaurants, and snack bars offering a range of foods and drinks, from light snacks to substantial dinners.

- Safety: Although guest happiness and safety are Parque Norte's top priorities, guests should abide by the given rules and regulations, particularly when utilizing the water slides or engaging in sporting activities. Park employees and lifeguards are on hand to help visitors and make sure they have a fun and safe time.

- Accessibility: The park makes an effort to provide wheelchair-accessible spaces, ramps, and paved walkways for guests of all ages and abilities. When they arrive, guests with specific requirements or mobility issues may ask about accommodations or help.

A favorite spot for both residents and visitors, Parque Norte provides a lively mix of outdoor leisure, family-friendly events, and aquatic experiences. Whether swimming, playing sports with friends, or just relaxing in the sun, guests visiting Medellin are certain to have a great time at Parque Norte.

CHAPTER 4: FOOD AND DRINKS

Medellin 's Cocktail Tour

The Cocktail Tour in Medellin provides guests with a special chance to see the city's exciting nightlife scene while enjoying a range of specialty cocktails and local libations. The trip, which is conducted by informed experts, takes guests on a tour of some of Medellin's best pubs, lounges, and nightclubs where they can have masterfully mixed cocktails, discover regional mixology methods, and take in the vibrant ambiance of the city. The Cocktail Tour highlights the richness and inventiveness of Medellin's cocktail culture, offering everything from traditional drinks with a Colombian touch to inventive concoctions inspired by regional cuisines. It's an unforgettable experience for both nightlife enthusiasts and lovers of cocktails.

Specialty Cocktails
1. Aguardiente: The national spirit of Colombia, aguardiente is a must-try during every trip to Medellin. Aguardiente, a powerful anise-flavored liquor made from sugarcane, is often consumed alone or combined with other alcoholic beverages. For a flavor of Colombian culture, seek for pubs and clubs that serve aguardiente-based beverages like the well-known "Aguardiente Sour" or "Aguardiente Mojito".

2. Lulada: A delicious drink prepared from lulo fruit, lime juice, sugar, and ice, originating in the Valle del Cauca area. Luladas, which have a tangy and lemony taste, are a popular option for those looking for something light and fruity to sip on during Medellin's warm nights. Seek out taverns and eateries that provide just Colombian food to experience this local staple.

3. Canelazo: Made with aguardiente, cinnamon, panela (raw cane sugar), and agua de panela (sugarcane water), canelazo is a warm and cozy drink that's ideal for winter evenings. During the colder months in Medellin, canelazo is a popular option, served hot and providing a delightful combination of spicy,

sweet, and alcoholic tastes. For a taste of traditional Colombian drinks this winter, seek for pubs and cafés that serve them.

4. Guaro Sour: A popular distilled spirit created from sugar cane, guaro, is used as the base liquor in this Colombian spin on the traditional Pisco Sour, which is a popular drink. The Guaro Sour, which combines fresh lime juice, simple syrup, and egg white, has a creamy texture and a smooth, zesty taste profile that makes it ideal for drinking while interacting with locals at Medellin's hip clubs and lounges.

Locations

1. El Poblado: This district is well-known for its exciting nightlife and is home to a large number of pubs, clubs, and cocktail lounges where guests may partake in a variety of beverages and entertainment choices. Discover well-liked locations like Carmen, Envy Rooftop, and Dulce Jesus Mio—known for their inventive drinks and vibrant atmosphere—by strolling around avenues like Parque Lleras and Provenza.

2. La 70: Situated in the Laureles area, La 70 is a busy boulevard with a local, more laid-back vibe thanks to its row of eateries, pubs, and bars. Tourists may explore the neighborhood's genuine charm and vibrant atmosphere by moving between different establishments and trying their signature drinks such as the Lulada and Canelazo.

3. Located on the banks of the Medellin River, Barrio Colombia is a well-liked area for nightlife because of its posh pubs, clubs, and entertainment establishments. When drinking drinks at stylish venues like Bendito Seas, Social Club, and Kukaramakara—where live music, DJs, and dancing

add to the excitement—visitors may take in the city's glitzy side.

4. The core of Medellin's nightlife, Parque Lleras is home to a wide variety of clubs, lounges, and cocktail lounges that can accommodate any kind of taste or desire. Explore the streets around the park to discover neighborhood favorites and hidden treasures like Alambique, La Octava, and Salon Amador, where talented mixologists create creative concoctions in chic surroundings.

Take the Medellin Cocktail Tour to see the city's most delicious cocktails and exciting nightlife destinations, where each drink has a backstory and every location delivers a unique experience that is not to be missed. To a fantastic voyage through Medellin's cocktail culture, cheers!

Medellin's Regional Food

Rich and varied, Medellin's food scene offers a mouthwatering range of tastes and ingredients inspired by regional delicacies and Colombian customs. Here are some of the best local dishes to sample in Medellin, ranging from filling stews and street snacks to unusual fruits and sweet treats:

1. Bandeja Paisa: Originally from the Antioquia province, whose capital is Medellin, this substantial and decadent feast is regarded as the national cuisine of Colombia. Grilled steak or pig, rice, beans, chorizo sausage, fried plantain, avocado, arepa (corn cake), crispy pork belly, and a fried egg are usually found on this filling dish. This substantial dinner represents the area's appreciation of robust food and agricultural background. It is delicious and fulfilling.

2. Sancocho: Popular across Colombia, particularly Medellin, Sancocho is a healthy and soothing soup. Simmered gently to generate rich tastes and soft textures, sancocho is made with a range of meats (such chicken, beef, or fish), root vegetables (including cassava, plantain, and potato), maize, and herbs. It's often served with avocado and a side of rice, which completes the meal and makes it feel extra good on chilly days.

3. Arepa: In Medellin as in other parts of Colombia, arepas are a basic meal. These round, thick maize cakes are great as an all-purpose snack or as a complement to a variety of dishes. They may be baked, fried, or grilled. Arepas provide many opportunities for personalization and taste combinations as they may be filled or topped with a variety of ingredients, including cheese, pork, beans, avocado, or eggs.

4. Lechona: A classic cuisine from the Tolima area that is appreciated all across Colombia, especially Medellin, is lechona. It is made out of a whole roasted pig that has been filled with rice, peas, onions, and spices. The result is a delicious meal with crispy skin and soft flesh. Lechona is a joyful and decadent delicacy that is often offered at special events and festivals.

5. Empanadas: Deep-fried till golden and crispy, empanadas are delicious turnovers packed with a variety of ingredients including cheese, meat, potatoes, or veggies. Empanadas are a common street food snack eaten anytime of the day in Medellin. They are a tasty and portable snack choice that may be purchased at bakeries, food booths, and local markets.

6. Ajiaco: Ajiaco is a classic Colombian soup prepared in a savory broth with chicken, three kinds of potatoes (including papas criollas, a little yellow potato), corn, and herbs. For lunch or supper, ajiaco is usually served with rice, avocado, and a dollop of cream, which makes for a hearty and filling dish.

7. Chicharrón: A common snack and garnish in Colombian cooking, chicharrón is crispy-fried pig belly or hog rind. Chicharrón is a popular topping for arepas and bandeja paisa in Medellin. It gives savory meals a rich, crispy taste. In addition, it's often served as a stand-alone snack with lime wedges and chili sauce for dipping.

8. Buñuelos: A combination of maize flour, cheese, eggs, and butter, these golden-fried dough balls have a light, fluffy texture with a subtle sweetness from the cheese. These addicting treats are often consumed warm and served warm with a drizzle of syrup or a dusting of powdered sugar for added decadence during holidays and celebratory events.

9. Cholado: Shaved ice, fresh fruit (mango, pineapple, banana, and strawberry), condensed milk, fruit syrup, and sometimes coconut flakes or marshmallows are combined to create this colorful and delicious treat. A famous street food snack in Medellin, this sweet and tangy dish provides a refreshing break from the tropical heat of the city.

10. Morcilla: Also known as blood sausage, morcilla is a traditional Colombian treat cooked with rice, onions, pig blood, and spices. It is then wrapped in a natural casing and usually fried or grilled until crispy. Morcilla, which has a distinctive blend of savory tastes and substantial textures, is eaten as a solitary snack or as part of traditional dinners in Medellin.

These are just a few of the mouthwatering and varied delicacies you may savor while discovering Medellin's gastronomic treasures. Your taste buds will be pleased by the tastes of Medellin's native cuisines whether you choose to indulge in traditional meals at family-owned restaurants, sample street snacks at local markets, or relish creative interpretations of Colombian cuisine at premium diners.

Medellin Wine Tour

Despite the fact that Colombia may not be well recognized for making wine, Medellin provides a distinctive wine tour experience that includes a variety of locally made wines in addition to foreign types. With the assistance of informed guides, guests can experience the best wine bars, vineyards, and tasting rooms in Medellin. The tour offers an opportunity to discover various wine regions, discover Colombian wine culture, and savor a wide range of fine wines matched with delectable cuisine. The Medellin Wine Tour provides an unforgettable and enlightening experience for everyone, regardless of whether they are wine enthusiasts, inquisitive tourists, or just wanting to relax and enjoy life's better pleasures.

Fantastic Wines
1. Vinos de Autor: Also known as "Author Wines," these artisanal wines are made by skilled winemakers in Colombia's wine-growing areas, including Valle del Cauca and Boyaca, using both conventional and novel winemaking methods. With varieties including Cabernet Sauvignon, Merlot, Chardonnay, and Sauvignon Blanc, these wines highlight the distinctive terroir of Colombia and provide a wide variety of flavors and textures to satisfy any palate.

2. Sparkling Wines: Colombia produces excellent sparkling wines due to its warm temperature and rich soils. These wines are great for commemorating special events or just to enjoy as an aperitif. Seek for Colombian sparkling wines produced using the classic techniques of Metodo Champenoise; styles

like Brut, Rosé, and Blanc de Blancs give sophisticated effervescence and a pleasant acidity.

3. Fruit Wines: Colombia is renowned for producing wonderful fruit wines from exotic tropical fruits including mango, passion fruit, guava, and pineapple in addition to grape-based wines. These fruit wines complement spicy food or sweets well since they have a blast of vivid flavors and aromas together with a touch of sweetness and acidity. Take the Medellin Wine Tour to sample a variety of fruit wines and discover the depth and diversity of Colombia's agricultural abundance.

4. foreign Wines: Medellin's wine tour provides the chance to sample a well chosen assortment of foreign wines from well-known wine-producing locations around the globe, even as Colombian wines continue to acquire popularity on a worldwide scale. Medellin's wine bars and tasting rooms provide a cosmopolitan ambiance while offering a wide variety of wines, from powerful reds from Argentina and Chile to crisp whites from Spain and Italy. Visitors may discover new favorites and broaden their wine horizons.

Locations
1. Barrio Provenza: A district in El Poblado, Barrio Provenza is home to a number of luxury wine bars and bistros where guests may unwind with a glass of wine in a chic, urban atmosphere. Discover well-known wineries like Vinoteca, Boca Grande, and Carmen Restaurant & Wine Bar by exploring avenues like Calle 10 and Calle 11. These establishments provide a wide variety of Colombian and foreign wines matched with fine dining options.

2. Envigado: Situated just south of Medellin, Envigado is home to a growing number of enotecas and wine bars offering a wide selection of both domestic and foreign wines. Experience the relaxed atmosphere and warm hospitality of places like La Vinoteca de Envigado or Bodega Barrio as you savor Colombian wines matched with tapas-style meals or handmade cheeses.

3. Valle del Cauca vineyards: One of Colombia's best wine-producing regions, the Valle del Cauca region is a day excursion from Medellin that offers a more in-depth wine experience. In the middle of picturesque scenery and undulating hills, you can visit wineries and vineyards like Viñedo Casa Santiago, Viña Sicilia, and San Vicente. Here, you can take a tour of the vineyards, discover how wine is made, and have samples of award-winning Colombian wines.

4. Wine Tasting Events: Medellin offers a variety of festivals, wine tasting events, and pop-up markets where you may taste a broad selection of wines from both domestic and foreign producers in one easy-to-find place. Keep an eye out for these events. These gatherings provide a fun and engaging opportunity to try new wines and meet other wine lovers. They often include live music, culinary pairings, and informative talks.

Take the Medellin Wine Tour to see the city's best wineries and tasting rooms while taking in the mouthwatering cuisine and learning about Colombia's rich tastes, varied terroirs, and dynamic wine culture. A memorable experience of Colombia's emerging wine sector awaits you on the Medellin Wine Tour, which will tantalize your senses whether you're seeing rural vineyards or enjoying sparkling wines in a stylish wine bar. To a memorable wine journey in Medellin, cheers!

CHAPTER 5: BEAUTY AND HEALTH

Medellin Beauty and Spa

There are several spa and beauty facilities in Medellin where guests may enjoy relaxing spa treatments, restorative massages, and expert salon services. Medellin's spa and beauty scene has something for everyone, whether you're in need of a fashionable hair makeover, a rejuvenating facial, or a soothing massage. Here are a few of the best spas and beauty parlors in the area:

1. Ocio Spa
- Spa Ocio is a peaceful haven in the center of Medellin, offering a variety of holistic therapies and wellness programs to encourage rest and renewal. Spa Ocio provides individualized experiences catered to each guest's requirements, ranging from therapeutic massages and body cleanses to facials and cosmetic treatments.
- Address: 43A #11A-15 Carrera, Medellin, Antioquia, Colombia

2. Spa Aguamia
- Aguamia Spa specializes on opulent spa treatments that mix traditional therapeutic methods with contemporary conveniences. Before enjoying a range of massage therapies, body wraps, and beauty treatments, guests may rest in the spa's steam rooms, jacuzzis, and relaxation zones.
- Address: Medellin, Antioquia, Colombia; Calle 10 # 35-08

3. Glow Spa
- Description: Glow Spa focuses on natural and organic treatments to improve both inner and outward attractiveness, offering a holistic approach to beauty and wellbeing. Offerings include manicures, pedicures, facials, massages, and waxing, all done by licensed professionals in a calm and caring setting.
- Address: Medellin, Antioquia, Colombia; Carrera 37 #8A-52

4. Medellin's Beauty Lounge

- Description: Offering a comprehensive variety of beauty treatments for both men and women, The Beauty Lounge Medellin is a stylish and contemporary salon. The team of skilled specialists at the salon guarantees that customers leave feeling rejuvenated and confident, offering services ranging from haircuts and styling to nail care and cosmetics application.
- Address: Medellin, Antioquia, Colombia; Calle 8 #43B-21

5. Hamman Spa
- Description: Drawing inspiration from ancient Turkish baths, Hamman Spa provides an opulent and immersive spa experience. Indulgent services like body wraps, massages, and exfoliating scrubs are available, along with steam rooms, hot tubs, and relaxation zones.
Location: Medellin, Antioquia, Colombia; Carrera 43F #11B-04

6. Bella Spa
- Bella Spa offers a wide variety of spa and salon treatments intended to enhance beauty and wellbeing from head to toe. A revitalizing facial, a deep tissue massage, or a beautiful makeover—the team of professionals at Bella Spa is committed to going above and beyond your expectations.
Location: Medellin, Antioquia, Colombia; Carrera 38 # 10-68

7. Vital Spa
- Description: To promote harmony and balance, Vital Spa combines Eastern and Western treatment practices in a comprehensive approach to wellbeing. Energy healing, reflexology, aromatherapy, and acupuncture are among the services offered; all are carried out in a calm and caring setting.
- Address: Calle 11 # 43A-18, Antioquia, Colombia; Medellin

8. opulent Medellin spa
- Luxurious Spa Medellin provides an exceptional spa experience emphasizing customized care and meticulous attention to detail. A variety of decadent treatments, including massages, body scrubs, facials, and salon services, is available for guests to choose from. All treatments are provided in an opulent and peaceful environment.
- Address: Medellin, Antioquia, Colombia; Carrera 35 #7-52

These are just a few of the best spas and beauty parlors in Medellin where guests may unwind, revive, and savor indulgent treatments.

Medellin Fitness and Gym Facilities

With a wide range of gyms and training facilities for both residents and tourists, Medellin has a thriving fitness scene. These gyms provide cutting-edge facilities, knowledgeable trainers, and a friendly atmosphere, whether you're trying to stick to your training regimen while traveling or seeking professional advice to reach your fitness objectives. Here are a few of Medellin's best fitness facilities and gyms:

1. Bodytech
- Bodytech is a reputable network of fitness centers with many sites throughout Medellin. To meet all fitness levels, each facility provides a variety of group fitness programs, weight training equipment, and cardio machines. In addition, Bodytech offers personal training services and facilities including parking, showers, and locker rooms.
- Location: El Poblado, Laureles, and Envigado, among other places in Medellin.

2. Convenient Fit
- Smart Fit is an affordable fitness franchise that has locations in Medellin and other cities in Colombia. Smart Fit offers a range of exercise courses taught by professional teachers, contemporary equipment, and large training facilities all at a reasonable price. Flexible memberships give you access to every Smart Fit facility in the country.
- Location: El Poblado, Laureles, and Belen, among other places in Medellin.

3. Athletic City
Sport City is a high-end training facility and sports club that provides its members with an all-inclusive exercise experience. Sport City offers modern gym equipment, group exercise courses, and other amenities including tennis courts, swimming pools, and spas. There are personal trainers on hand to provide customized exercise plans and assistance.
- Location: Medellin, Antioquia, Colombia; Carrera 43A # 1 Sur 100

4. Altair Gimnasio
- Description: Situated in Medellin's Laureles district, Gimnasio Altair is a local gym. Compared to bigger chains, this boutique gym provides a more private atmosphere, individualized care, and a functional training emphasis. Gimnasio Altair has weightlifting and cardio equipment in addition to boxing, Pilates, and yoga courses.
Location: Medellin, Antioquia, Colombia; Circular 74b # 39-26

5. Life Fitness Center
- Description: Suitable for people of all ages and fitness levels, Life Fitness Gym is an expansive and well-equipped workout facility. Along with a variety of cardio, strength, and functional

training equipment, the gym also provides group exercise classes and coach-led personal training sessions.
Location: Medellin, Antioquia, Colombia; Carrera 76 # 48A-45

6. Fit 4 Less
- Fit 4 Less is a low-cost fitness franchise that provides membership alternatives at reasonable prices without sacrificing quality. Fit 4 Less offers a range of cardio machines, weight equipment, and group fitness sessions with an emphasis on accessibility and inclusion to assist members reach their fitness goals in a motivating setting.
- Address: Medellin, Antioquia, Colombia; Calle 10 # 34-11

7. Center of Spine
- Description: Indoor cycling sessions are the only focus of Spinning Center, a specialist exercise facility. The high-intensity exercises at Spinning Center, led by qualified instructors, are intended to increase endurance, burn calories, and enhance cardiovascular health. All skill levels of cyclists may find a stimulating and exciting atmosphere in the studio.
Location: Medellin, Antioquia, Colombia; Carrera 41 # 10-26

8. CrossFit Medellin
- Description: CrossFit Medellin is a CrossFit affiliate facility that offers intense, dynamic workouts built on functional movements. Members may enhance their strength, endurance, and general fitness with the assistance of the gym's skilled trainers, who provide individualized advice and professional teaching. In addition, CrossFit Medellin provides seminars and specialized training.
Location: Medellin, Antioquia, Colombia; Carrera 76 # 48A-45

These are only a few of the best fitness facilities and gyms in Medellin where guests can maintain an active lifestyle while visiting the city. To assist you reach your fitness objectives, Medellin's fitness facilities provide a range of alternatives, including group fitness classes, specialist training programs, and standard gym routines.

CHAPTER 6: MEDELLIN ITINERARY FOR 7 DAYS

Day 1: Welcome and Overview of Medellin
Morning:
- Get to Medellin and make sure your lodging is ready.
- Savor a leisurely breakfast at a restaurant or café in the area.

- To get acquainted with the neighborhood and its highlights, take a walking tour of El Poblado.

In the afternoon:
- See Fernando Botero's renowned sculptures in Plaza Botero.
- Discover the variety of plant species found at Medellin's Botanical Garden.
- Enjoy a fresh and healthful meal at one of the garden's cafés for lunch.

Evening:
- For supper and nightlife, visit El Poblado's Parque Lleras.
- Pick from a range of eateries offering foreign and Colombian food.
- Visit a bar or club in Parque Lleras to take advantage of live music and cocktails while taking in Medellin's lively nightlife.

Day 2: Investigation of Cultures
Morning:
- Visit the Museo de Antioquia first thing in the morning to get knowledge about the history and culture of the area.
- Take pictures with the enormous statues and explore the Plaza Botero area.

In the afternoon:
- Join a guided tour of Comuna 13 to see how community initiatives and street art have transformed the neighborhood. Lunch at a neighborhood eatery in Comuna 13 and try some typical Colombian fare.

Evening:
- Go back to El Poblado and unwind over supper at a quaint eatery.

- Take into consideration going to a local live music or cultural event.

Day 3: Nature Exploration
Morning:
- For breathtaking views of the city and the surrounding mountains, spend a day in Parque Arvi and ride the Metrocable.
- Take a hike on one of the park's paths or hire a bike to enjoy a beautiful ride through the forest.

In the afternoon:
- Enjoy a picnic lunch in Parque Arvi's scenic surroundings.

Evening:
- Go back to Medellin and relax at a nearby wellness facility with a massage or spa treatment.
- Try a casual eatery in the area or have a peaceful evening at your lodging.

Day 4: The Culture of Coffee
Morning:
- Go on a guided trip of a local coffee plantation to see how coffee is produced in Colombia.
- Take part in a coffee tasting event and try several brews.

In the afternoon:
- At the coffee plantation, have a typical Colombian meal.

Evening:
- Go back to Medellin and explore the food scene of the city in the evening.
- For evening, choose a place that specializes in Colombian food and pair it with a glass of regional wine or artisan beer.

Day 5: leisure and shopping
Morning:
- Shop for trinkets and handcrafted goods in one of Medellin's lively marketplaces, such Mercado del Rio or Mercado de San Alejo.

In the afternoon:
- Take use of the facilities and activities of Parque Norte or Parque Explora to pass the day leisurely.

Evening:
- Indulge in cutting-edge food and premium wines for a gourmet supper at one of Medellin's elegant restaurants.
- Consider your travels so far and plan your last days in Medellin.

Day 6: Adventure and Nature
Morning:
- Set off on a day excursion to Piedra del Peñol, where you may climb the recognizable rock structure to get sweeping views of the surroundings.

In the afternoon:
- Savor lunch in the quaint village of Guatape, which is well-known for its seaside promenade and colorful houses.

Evening:
- Go back to Medellin and spend the evening discovering what the Laureles district has to offer at night.
- Stop by a neighborhood pub or brewery to try some artisan brews and socialize with other tourists and locals.

Day 7: Leaving and Saying Goodbye

Morning:

Savor your last breakfast at your lodging while taking in the end of your time in Medellin.

- Take one last walk around the area to take in the city's sights and noises.

In the afternoon:

- Vacate your lodging and make your way to the airport in time for your flight out.
- Consider the adventures you had in Medellin and begin organizing your next trip.

Evening:

- Leave Medellin with happy memories and a fresh understanding of this energetic metropolis.

CHAPTER 7: MEDELLIN WEATHER AND CAMPING

The weather pattern in Medellin

Travelers looking for moderate temperatures and outdoor activities will find Medellin, often known as the "City of

Eternal Spring," to have a lovely year-round climate. Here is a thorough guide about Medellin's weather trends to assist travelers in making travel plans:

Seasons:
1. Dry Season (December to February, June to August): Medellin has two dry seasons: June to August and December to February. The weather is usually bright and dry throughout these months, with little likelihood of rain. During the day, temperatures vary from 22°C to 28°C (72°F to 82°F), which is ideal for outdoor sports and tourism.

2. Rainy Season (March to May, September to November): March to May and September to November are the dates of Medellin's rainy seasons. Although there is more rainfall in these months, it generally occurs in the afternoon or evening in brief spurts, leaving the mornings mostly dry. The temperature stays comfortable, ranging from 20°C to 26°C (68°F to 79°F), with a few nights that are colder.

Overview of the Monthly Weather:
- January through March: These months, which include warm, bright days, signal the start of the dry season. Still, there's a chance of afternoon rains, so bring an umbrella or a rain jacket.
- April to June: April marks the start of the rainy season, which is characterized by higher rainfall and sporadic thunderstorms. Mornings are often bright and nice for outdoor activities, even in the rain.
- July through September: This time of year is marked by chilly temps and sporadic downpours. The weather is still pleasant enough to explore the city and its environs, however.
- October to December: In October, the rainy season ends, and in November and December, the weather becomes drier again.

Sunny days and chilly nights are to be expected, making the weather ideal for outdoor activities and tourism.

Microclimates and Altitude:
The altitude and microclimates in Medellin and the neighboring areas may affect the city's weather. Although the city center has a moderate climate, locations at higher elevations may have more precipitation and colder temperatures. When visiting neighboring towns or tourist destinations, visitors should be ready for sudden weather changes.

Packing Advice:
- Lightweight summertime apparel, such as T-shirts, shorts, and breathable materials.
- A lightweight sweater or jacket for chilly nights, particularly in the rainy season.
- Comfy walking shoes to explore the uneven topography of the city.
- Sunscreen, hats, and sunglasses to shield yourself from the sun's rays.
- A raincoat or umbrella in case of sudden downpours, particularly during the wet season.

Camping In Medellin

Advice for Medellin Campers
1. Examine Campsites: Prior to leaving on your camping vacation, do some research and choose a location that best meets your requirements and tastes. Take into account elements like accessibility, amenities, and location.

2. Examine Weather Forecasts: Although Medellin has good weather most of the year round, it is still important to check

the weather prediction before going camping. During the rainy season, be ready for possible downpours and pack appropriately.

3. Pack Light: To reduce the weight of your bag while camping in Medellin, try to just carry the necessities. When choosing clothes and equipment for camping, take the terrain and temperature into account.

4. Honor Nature: Adhere to the Leave No Trace philosophy and show consideration for the surrounding ecosystem. Make sure to properly dispose of rubbish, reduce noise pollution, and keep animals from being disturbed.

5. Keep Hydrated: It's important to remain hydrated while camping in Medellin because of the city's often warm and muggy weather. Drink plenty of water throughout the day, particularly if you're doing outside activities.

6. Carry insect repellent: Insects, including mosquitoes, may be encountered, especially in forested regions or close to water sources. Carry bug repellant to protect yourself from stings and bites.

7. Plan Your Meals in Ahead: To guarantee you have enough food for your camping trip, plan and prepare your meals ahead of time. Think about simple-to-prepare, lightweight, non-perishable solutions.

8. Pack the Right Shoes: Select supportive and comfortable shoes that are appropriate for strolling and trekking on a variety of surfaces. To avoid blisters and pain, make sure your shoes are broken in before heading out on a camping trip.

9. Remain Organized: Store your camping goods and equipment neatly in your tent or bag so you can find what you need when you need it. Sort and safeguard your valuables using storage bags or partitions.

10. Notify Others of Your Plans: Before leaving for a camping trip, let your loved ones know about your schedule, including the campground you want to use and when you anticipate to return. In the event of an emergency, this guarantees that someone is aware of your location.

Essentials for a Medellin camping trip
Camping Equipment:
- Tent
- A sleeping bag
- A cushion or bed mattress
- Fuel and stove for camping
- Cooking implements
- A carry-around lantern or flashlight
- A knife or multitool
- Foldable chairs or camp chairs

Clothes and Sneakers:
- Breathable and light apparel
- Long-sleeved clothing to defend against the sun
- A poncho or waterproof jacket
- A cap or hat to shield against the sun
Sturdy walking shoes or hiking boots
- Extra underwear and socks

Personal Requirements:
- First Aid Package
- Sunscreen
- Repellent for insects

- Toiletries, such as soap that decomposes naturally
- Prescription drugs
- Information about emergency contacts and personal identity

Accessories for the outdoors:
A daypack or a backpack
- A stuff bag or camping pillow packed with clothing
- Hiking poles, if applicable
- A pair of binoculars
- A smartphone or camera to record memories

Food and Hydration:
Water containers or hydration packs
- Filtration systems or tablets for water purification
- High-energy nibbles (granola bars, trail mix)
- Freeze-dried or dehydrated food
- Ingredients for cooking (rice, pasta, canned foods)

Amusement and Coziness:
- Books or electronic readers
- Engaging in card games or trip games
- Instruments of music (if wanted)
- Headphones or a portable speaker
- A portable hammock or chair for camping

Security and Emergencies:
- Compass and map or GPS gadget
- A whistle
- An emergency cover or cave
- A firestarting device (firesteel, matches, or lighter).
A stockpile of food and water for many days
- Local emergency numbers and emergency contact details

These camping advice and a list of must-haves will help you have a safe and enjoyable time in Medellin's stunning natural surroundings. Be ready, be mindful of the environment, and enjoy your camping experience whether you're in the mountains, next to a waterfall, or by a serene lake.

CHAPTER 8 : SIMPLE LANGUAGE PHRASES TO KNOW IN MEDELLIN

Greetings
- Hola: Hello

- Buenos días: Good morning
- Buenas tardes: Good afternoon
- Buenas noches: Good evening
- ¿Cómo estás?: How are you?
- Mucho gusto: Nice to meet you
- Adiós: Goodbye

Basic Phrases

- Sí: Yes
- No: No
- Por favor: Please
- Gracias: Thank you
- De nada: You're welcome
- Lo siento: I'm sorry
- ¿Cómo se dice... en español?: How do you say... in Spanish?

Asking for Directions

- ¿Dónde está...?: Where is...?
- ¿Cómo llego a...?: How do I get to...?
- ¿Puede ayudarme?: Can you help me?
- ¿Cuánto tiempo se tarda?: How long does it take?

Ordering Food and Drinks

- Quisiera...: I would like...
- ¿Qué recomienda?: What do you recommend?
- La cuenta, por favor: The check, please
- ¿Tienen menú en inglés?: Do you have a menu in English?

Making Requests

- ¿Podría...?: Could you...?
- ¿Puedo tener...?: Can I have...?
- Por favor, hable más despacio: Please speak more slowly
- Me puede repetir, por favor?: Can you repeat that, please?

Getting Around

- ¿Dónde está la estación de metro?: Where is the metro station?
- ¿Cómo llego al centro?: How do I get to downtown?
- ¿Hay un taxi cerca?: Is there a taxi nearby?
- ¿Cuánto cuesta el pasaje?: How much is the fare?

Shopping

- ¿Cuánto cuesta esto?: How much does this cost?
- ¿Tienen esto en otro color/talla?: Do you have this in another color/size?
- Me gustaría comprar esto: I would like to buy this
- ¿Aceptan tarjeta de crédito?: Do you accept credit cards?

Learning these simple language phrases will help you navigate Medellin more comfortably and interact with locals with ease.

CONCLUSION

As the journey through the captivating city of Medellin draws to a close, we reflect on the vibrant tapestry of experiences woven within its colorful streets. From the bustling markets and historic landmarks to the lush greenery and majestic mountains that frame the city, Medellin has captured our hearts and ignited our sense of adventure.

Throughout this travel guide, we've embarked on a whirlwind exploration of Medellin's rich culture, diverse cuisine, and breathtaking natural beauty. We've wandered through bustling plazas adorned with the iconic sculptures of Fernando Botero, delved into the city's tumultuous history at Museo de Antioquia, and savored the flavors of Colombian coffee on a picturesque mountainside.

But beyond the tangible attractions lies something truly magical – the warmth and hospitality of the people of Medellin. From the cheerful greetings of locals in the streets to the genuine kindness extended by shopkeepers and restaurant owners, Medellin welcomes visitors with open arms and leaves an indelible mark on their souls.

As we bid farewell to this enchanting city, let us carry with us the memories of sun-drenched days and starlit nights, of laughter shared with newfound friends and moments of quiet reflection amidst nature's embrace. Medellin has bestowed upon us a gift – the gift of discovery, of connection, and of endless possibility.

So, whether you're a seasoned traveler or a first-time adventurer, may the spirit of Medellin continue to inspire and guide you on your journey through life. And as you turn the final page of this guide, remember that the memories we've made here are just the beginning of a lifetime of exploration and discovery.

Farewell, dear reader, and may your next adventure be as vibrant and unforgettable as the city of Medellin itself. Until we meet again, ¡Hasta luego!

Made in the USA
Las Vegas, NV
29 September 2024

95970019R00063